Mashiach

מָשִׁיחַ

D. A. Osterman

D.A. Osterman

Mashiach

Requests for permission to make copies of any part of the work should be submitted to the publisher, Ashkenazi Press: davidcohen7891@gmail.com

Published by: Ashkenazi Press
a subsidiary of The ITM Group

ASHKENAZI
PRESS

ISBN-10: 0692457798
ISBN-13: 978-0692457795
First Edition
Date of Publication: July 1, 2015

Printed in the United States of America
CreateSpace, Charleston SC

Front Cover Photo: © Photo.UA | Shutterstock
Rear Cover Photo: © Shoham | Wikimedia Commons

Mashiach

About the Cover Photos

Front Cover Photo: © Photo.UA | Shutterstock

The Golden Gate, is the oldest of the current gates in Jerusalem's Old City Walls. According to Jewish tradition, the Shekhinah (שכינה) (Divine Presence) used to appear through this gate, and will appear again when Mashiach comes and a new gate replaces the present one; that is why Jews used to pray for mercy at the former gate at this location.

Ottoman Sultan Suleiman the Magnificent, sealed off the Golden Gate as shown on the cover in 1541 C.E. thinking he could prevent Mashiach's entrance.

Rear Cover Photo: © Shoham | Wikimedia Commons

"Inside the Golden Gate" by Yaakov Shoham (Own work (own picture)) [Public domain], via Wikimedia Commons.

D.A. Osterman

Dedication

This book is dedicated to:

The G-d of

Abraham, Isaac, and Jacob

Thanks to all of my family and friends who
have invested hours reviewing and
proofreading this book.

Extra Special thanks to my friend

Simon Stout in Tel Aviv,

and to my best friend on Earth,

Joyce

She truly is my Proverbs 31 wife.

Mashiach

Complete Jewish Bible

Copyright © 1998 by David H. Stern

Throughout the Mashiach all passage quotations from the Tanakh, are from the Complete Jewish Bible (CJB) unless otherwise noted. The CJB was translated by David H. Stern, an Isra'el-based Jewish theologian. It was first published in 1998, in what both David Stern calls "… in the Jewish manner and presentation." The names of the books are Jewish, along with their English names. Semitic names are used for people and places. The author also incorporates Hebrew and Yiddish expressions that Stern refers to as "Jewish English."

The Complete Jewish Bible Tanakh is a paraphrase of the 1917 Jewish Publication Society version of the Tanakh (also known as the Masoretic Text). The CJB is a free translation, with Yiddish and modern Jewish cultural expressions. Stern claims his purpose for producing the Complete Jewish Bible was "to restore G-d's Word to its original Jewish context and culture as well as be in easy to read modern English."

Because of the primacy of Scripture, Tanakh passages are incorporated as often as possible, and numerous other references to Scripture are generally listed in line.

D.A. Osterman

When One Door of Happiness Closes, Another Opens; But Often We Look So Long At The Closed Door That We Do Not See The One Which Has Been Opened For Us.

-- Helen Keller

Mashiach

Chapter 1
A Unifying Hope

A unifying hope of the Tanakh is the coming of Mashiach and the establishment of the Kingdom of G-d among humanity. One purpose of this book is to review with an open mind and discuss the contents of these prophecies about Mashiach. Let's start with a quote from a passage about Mashiach in the Tanakh book of Malachi 3:1-6:

> Look! I am sending my messenger to clear the way before me; and the L-rd, whom you seek, will suddenly come to his temple. Yes, the messenger of the covenant, in whom you take such delight — look! Here he comes, says Adonai-Tzva'ot. But who can endure the day when he comes? Who can stand when he appears? For he will be like a refiner's fire,

like the soap maker's lye. He will sit, testing and purifying the silver; he will purify the sons of Levi, refining them like gold and silver, so that they can bring offerings to Adonai uprightly.

Then the offering of Y'hudah and Yerushalayim will be pleasing to Adonai, as it was in the days of old, as in years gone by. 'Then I will approach you for judgment; and I will be quick to witness against sorcerers, adulterers and perjurers; against those who take advantage of wage-earners, widows and orphans; against those who rob the foreigner of his rights and don't fear me,' says Adonai-Tzva'ot. 'But because I, Adonai, do not change, you sons of Ya'akov will not be destroyed.'   -- Malachi 3:1-6 (CJB)

The discussion of Mashiach between Jews and Christians has been controversial and sometimes emotional. However, one thing is clear from the above reading. The Messenger of the Covenant, our Mashiach, will appear to humanity. Then he will sit in his temple, judge people, and punish the judged: "Then I will approach you for judgment." Where will we be spiritually as we stand before Him?

Another purpose of this book is to reveal both new and old ideas concerning Mashiach and to provoke the reader to new thoughts about him. There are many

Mashiach

scholarly books and papers written on the subject, but most academics who have written on the appearance of our Mashiach write for each other and not for the ordinary reader. I seek to accomplish a thought-provoking book on the Mashiach for the average person, and to let the truth and beauty of Tanakh and its way of life show the right path to finding Mashiach.

This book does not claim to be a complete investigation into all Jewish ideas, dogma, and thought about Mashiach. However, it does touch significantly on the prophecies foretelling his appearance on Earth. These prophesies are intended to provoke a desire to pursue a personal study and understanding of the term "Mashiach" as used by our ancient rabbinical forefathers. Can their teachings stand up to the test of fire when set alongside the prophets' prophesies?

The assumption throughout the book is that the reader has a basic understanding of the Torah which is the first 5 books of the twenty-four books of the Tanakh, or the Jewish Bible. The Tanakh presents a history of the first 3,500 years from creation until the building of the second Temple in Jerusalem. The books also relate the history of the Jewish nation from its earliest stage, through the giving of the Law at Mount Sinai, and until the end of the first commonwealth.

But the Tanakh is much more than just history. In it one can learn about G-d's plan for the world and of His relationship with mankind, specifically, His chosen nation the Jews.

There is no resource more important than a text of the Bible itself. If you can read Hebrew, it is best to read it in the original Hebrew; but at a minimum, one should at least refer to the original Hebrew to appreciate its nuances.

Here is where G-d tells us what He wants us to do:

> So now, Isra'el, all that Adonai your G-d asks from you is to fear Adonai your G-d, follow all his ways, love him and serve Adonai your G-d with all your heart and all your being; to obey, for your own good, the mitzvot and regulations of Adonai which I am giving you today.
> -- Deuteronomy 10: 12-13 (CJB)

The word "Torah" is a tricky one, because it can mean different things in different contexts. In its most limited sense, "Torah" refers to the Five Books of Moses: Genesis, Exodus, Leviticus, Numbers, and Deuteronomy. But the word "Torah" can also be used to refer to the entire Hebrew Bible. Most Jews today accept the use of the word "Tanakh" as a reference to the entire Jewish Bible, including the Torah. The author accepts this definition as well; however, in many (most) cases, the author refers to the Torah separately as these 5 books of Moses are the most important books in the Jewish bible.

Mashiach

Chapter 2
Mashiach Traditions - All or Nothing

While most would agree the central doctrine of the Torah and Tanakh Holy Books is G-d and his oneness as stated in the first commandment, the coming of Mashiach and the establishment of the Kingdom of G-d among the Jewish people is certainly an essential theme throughout these books. By many accounts there are several hundred prophecies about Mashiach in almost all the books of the Tanakh, beginning with the Torah and ending with the last prophets Zachariah and Malachi.

Today, most Jew's consider Mashiach to be primarily a political figure that will rescue Isra'el from war and terror. He will redeem everything that Isra'el and its people have lost over the decades and centuries while in exile. Based upon both our Abrahamic and Davidic Covenants, he will bring back the twelve Tribes, unifying Isra'el and establishing his rule in a purified Jerusalem.

Our traditions teach us that **all** of six of the following criteria **must** be fulfilled before any person can be acknowledged as the true Mashiach:

1. Building the 'Kingdom of G-d' creating a Worldwide Reign of Peace
2. Rebuilding of the Holy Temple
3. Ingathering of the Jewish Exiles
4. Observance of the Torah Embraced by All Jews
5. Universal Knowledge of G-d
6. Mashiach must be born of the Tribe of Judah and a Descendant of King David AND King Solomon.

Faith is irrelevant to the Jewish concept of the Mashiach ben David. An individual either fulfills all of these prophetic criteria or he doesn't; and he therefore cannot be Mashiach.

These six traditions are examined in the following chapters in some detail. While the Tanakh is filled with prophecies about Mashiach and his Kingdom, the Hebrew word Mashiach (מְשִׁיחַ) is extremely rare in the writings of the Prophets. This word is only found once in Isaiah, once in Lamentations, twice in Daniel, and once in Habakkuk. While that is the case, the original writers of the Tanakh were trying to prepare us Jews— and through us—all the world for the coming of Mashiach. Their desire was for us to recognize him and believe him when he arrives. It was a difficult task, because at the same time they were revealing the G-d

Mashiach

nature of Mashiach they could not contradict the Jewish belief in Adonai as the "One True G-d." They did not want to blur the lines into polytheism. Thus language to describe G-d's nature was difficult at best, not unlike trying to discern G-d's face in the burning bush! Yet, these prophets succeeded, consequently bestowing upon them titles as G-d's messengers.

The large number of prophecies in the Tanakh is proof of the existence of G-d. The mere fact that our prophets could foresee future occurrences hundreds and in some cases thousands of years before they actually happened shows that the only way this could have occurred was if G-d actually spoke to them and through them.

Mashiach is an essential doctrine in the Tanakh. However, one must acknowledge that the details of Tanakh prophecy are frequently encompassed by mystery. To speak with certainty about the meanings of these prophecies is a serious mistake and just guesswork no matter who is doing the guessing, even if espoused by serious and knowledgeable scholars, whether they are Rabbis or Jewish leaders or theology professors from leading universities. Many "experts" have narrowly focused on a particular perspective in their own belief system and insisted their philosophy is the only correct interpretation. This creates an obstacle between themselves and other Jewish brethren who hold another view or interpretation. Going far back in Jewish history, to the time of the Pharisees and scribes and the Jewish people of that time in Isra'el, even though they studied the Tanakh fastidiously, they had a difficult time understanding it.

One thing all these experts will agree upon is that Mashiach as prophesied will save and protect Isra'el. No one truly knows exactly when that will happen. It could be today, or it might be another 1,000 years. The truth has been purposefully shrouded in G-d's Tanakh prophecies so that no one can truly know when Mashiach will come. It is with this view that we will look into these six important doctrines of faith and Jewish tradition. Through in-depth research to understand the actual prophetic words in the Tanakh without interjecting theories and opinions, this author kept in mind that even the prophets who were G-d inspired to write their visions of future events were often not given the foreknowledge by G-d of the "who-what-where" relating to what G-d asked them to write and prophesy.

It is certainly fine to have firm beliefs about these prophecies, but we should not allow ourselves to be divided from our sincere brothers with whom there is a disagreement. Too many of our fellow Jews are antagonistic about what they believe. Too many Jews today separate themselves from other movements because of their own beliefs. As a people of G-d, whether Orthodox, Reform, Conservative, Hasidic or Kabbalah, we need to remember the Jewish tradition of humility as one of our greatest virtues. The opposite— pride—is one of our worst vices. We only have to look to Moses, the greatest of man, as our chief example. The Torah tells us in Numbers 12:3 (CJB), "Now this man Moshe was very humble, more so than anyone on earth." Yet he was able to muster the courage to confront Pharaoh, and at times even argue with G-d. Humility enables us to pull off our spiritual blinders in search of the truth, but pride shutters all doors; and basking in it, we will miss out on the greatest truths ever prophesied!

In varying degrees of importance to the various Jewish sects, tradition plays an important role in Judaism. A Jew investigating Mashiach might want to know what a 2nd century B.C.E. or 10th century C.E. Rabbi thought about a particular verse which sheds light on what the Tanakh says.

Throughout this book, the author has tried to understand the Tanakh meanings in their plainest literal (P'shat) sense by following the directive in the Talmud. The P'shat interpretive method is the practice rabbis generally prefer as specified in the Talmud, in Shabbat 63A: "A verse cannot depart from its plain meaning..."

The importance of this statement is revealed by Rabbi Aharon Feldman in his book, *The Juggler and the King*. Rabbi Feldman describes the comment, "a verse cannot depart from its plain meaning," as the "Sages dictum." A *dictum* is an "authoritative declaration." He goes on to say that it is an authoritative declaration of the rabbinic sages that "the simple meaning of the text is always true." Therefore, the rabbinic sages preferred the interpretive method as a manner of understanding the Tanakh.

It is also the preferred method used by most modern day biblical scholars, such as David L. Cooper's Golden Rule of Interpretation which states the following:

> When the plain sense of Scripture makes common sense, seek no other sense; therefore, take every word at its primary, ordinary, usual, literal meaning unless the facts of the immediate context, studied in the light of related passages and axiomatic and fundamental truths, indicate clearly otherwise.

In other words, if the Torah and the Tanakh give a straight forward explanation, the author is of the opinion that it should be accepted as the best interpretation unless there is some compelling reason in the actual text to indicate that the explanation is meant only symbolically. When the Torah or Tanakh makes plain sense as written, I see no reason to speculate or look elsewhere.

While this book is not a *Yeshiva* in the sense of the Hebrew word, meaning *sitting*, or, *sitting and meeting together*; I have tried to follow the traditional Jewish approach of the Socratic method of questions and answers.

Mashiach

Chapter 3
The Anointed One - Who is Mashiach?

Before we explore the six traditions of Mashiach, a discussion about *who is Mashiach* is appropriate. Simply put, Mashiach is the Hebrew word for "Messiah." The word *messiah* in English means, *a savior*, or, *a hoped-for deliverer*. The Hebrew for the word is "Mashiach," which means "the Anointed One," or if literally translated; "to smear" as with oil.

Anointing was done to set apart items and people to G-d's service. The Holy oil was made from a recipe given directly to Moses by G-d. The oil is made from a base of olive oil. The olive oil was to be pure, and nothing but pure because it represents the HOLY Spirit of YHWH. It was then compounded with a very special recipe of aromatic spices and then restricted for tabernacle use only. Anyone violating G-d's command for its purpose was put to death. This oil will be important when Mashiach appears. Yet, where is this special anointing oil? How will Mashiach be anointed

11

with it?

In Talmudic literature, the title Mashiach, or Melech HaMashiach (the King Mashiach), is reserved for the Jewish leader who will redeem Isra'el in the End Times.

G-d has promised Mashiach from the very beginning of the Torah and throughout the Tanakh. In fact, as the Tanakh unfolds, we realize it is a book of ever increasing anticipation of Mashiach. An example is in Genesis 3:15, where G-d promises that one of Eve's offspring will crush the head of the serpent. Another example is Isaiah, wherein G-d promises:

> For a child is born to us, a son is given to us; dominion will rest on his shoulders, and he will be given the name Pele-Yo'etz El Gibbor Avi-'Ad Sar-Shalom [Wonder of a Counselor, Mighty G-d, Father of Eternity, Prince of Peace], in order to extend the dominion and perpetuate the peace of the throne and kingdom of David, to secure it and sustain it through justice and righteousness henceforth and forever. The zeal of Adonai-Tzva'ot will accomplish this. -- Isaiah 9:6-7 (CJB)

Our prophets were given several of these partial revelations about the coming Mashiach. Just as today, the prophets wondered when and how our Mashiach would come. One popular belief has endured for centuries. The nation of Isra'el will quickly be raised above all others, returning G-d's Kingdom to the

Mashiach

Golden Age of David and Solomon, but under Mashiach. He is expected to bring military success and a regime that will crush conflicting nations while establishing global peace.

The Talmud tells many revelations about Mashiach, some of which represent famous Talmudic rabbis as receiving personal visitations from Elijah the Prophet and Mashiach. The book of Deuteronomy predicts the arrival of an "anointed one," or Mashiach who will "deliver" or "save" the Jewish people. He will be the very real king of a very real Torah government in the Land of Isra'el.

> Adonai will raise up for you a prophet like me from among yourselves, from your own kinsmen. You are to pay attention to him... I will put my words in his mouth, and he will tell them everything I order him. Whoever doesn't listen to my words, which he will speak in my name, will have to account for himself to me.
> -- Deuteronomy 18:15-19 (CJB)

The dominant Jewish messianic expectation today is one put forth by Rabbi Moshe ben Maimon ("Maimonides," 1138 - 1204 C.E.), a highly-respected medieval Jewish philosopher. His writings are considered by most Jews to be foundational to Jewish thought and study considering Mashiach. Maimonides is responsible for creating the thirteen tenets of the Jewish faith. His twelfth tenet in the Jewish faith

(Shloshah Asar Ikkarim) from his introduction to Chapter Helek of Mishna Torah is as follows:

> I believe with full faith in the coming of the Mashiach. And even though he tarries, with all that, I await his arrival with every day. No date must be fixed for his appearance, neither may the scriptures be interpreted with the view of deducing the time of his coming. The Sages said (Sanhedrin 97b), קצין מחשבי של רולן תפח A plague on those who calculate periods (for Messiah's appearance).

Despite our faith, there has been one "small" problem, however. In the Torah there are directions for anointing kings, in particular Mashiach. There is a very special mixture of the sacred oil of the anointing, ordered to be made in Exodus 30:22-33, for sanctification of religious articles and leaders as follows:

> Adonai said to Moshe, 'Take the best spices—500 shekels of myrrh [12 1/2 pounds], half this amount (250 shekels) of aromatic cinnamon [today called Cinnamon Persimmon] [6 1/4 pounds], 250 shekels of aromatic cane, 500 shekels of cassia (use the sanctuary standard), and one gallon of olive oil—and make them into a holy anointing oil; blend it and perfume it as would an expert perfume-maker; it will be a holy anointing oil. Use it to anoint the tent

Mashiach

of meeting, the ark for the testimony, the table and all its utensils, the menorah and all its utensils, the incense altar, the altar for burnt offerings and all its utensils, and the basin with its base. You are to consecrate them—they will be especially holy, and whatever touches them will be holy. Then you are to anoint Aharon and his sons—you are to consecrate them to serve me in the office of cohen.'

And:

Tell the people of Isra'el, 'This is to be holy anointing oil **for me** through **all your generations**. It is not to be used for anointing a person's body; and you are not to make any like it, with the same composition of ingredients—it is holy, and you are to treat it as holy. Whoever makes any like it or uses it on any unauthorized person is to be cut off from his people.'   -- Exodus 30:22-33 (CJB)

The Holy Anointing oil, Shemen Afarsimon also called, the Shemen Ha'Mishchah (שמן המשחה), formed an integral part of the Torah ordination of priests as well as consecrating of the articles of the Tabernacle. The main purpose of the holy anointing oil was to cause the anointed persons or objects to become ha'kodesh–most holy. It is said that the materials as specified exactly by G-d were to be followed exactly and any deviation would bring certain death.

D.A. Osterman

Originally, the oil was used exclusively for the priests and the Tabernacle articles, but was later extended to include prophets and kings (I Samuel 10:1). It was forbidden to be used on an outsider (Exodus 30:33), or to be used on the body of any common persons (Ex. 30:32a). The Isra'elites were forbidden to duplicate any like it for themselves (Ex. 30:32b).

Unfortunately, all of the official anointing oil stored at the Temple was lost in 70 C.E. as the Romans sacked Jerusalem and burned the Temple to the ground. Even if someone had been brave enough to make this oil, it was impossible. For the last 1900 years, one of the ingredients, the sap from the ancient orchards of a persimmon plant—very similar to today's Cinnamon persimmon plant—to remake this oil, is no longer available. Therefore, it's impossible to "officially" sanctify anyone or anything. Or is it? Perhaps the discovery of the special Persimmon plant, or even the oil, could signal Mashiach's arrival. Could either of these two be found?

This sap of the persimmon plant was particularly valuable in ancient times and had tremendous economic value to Judea because it held a sweet fragrance at a time when the ability to manufacture perfume was limited.

Roman historians recounted that in 70 C.E., when Titus's army marched toward Jericho and Ein Gedi to destroy Jerusalem and the second Jewish Temple, our Jewish ancestors tried to destroy the persimmon orchards to keep them out of Roman hands.

They failed in their attempt to destroy them, and

Mashiach

Titus's army is said to have waved persimmon plants as soldiers marched triumphantly back to Rome. Yet it is obvious G-d did not want the valuable ingredient for the Anointing Oil to fall into Roman hands, or for that matter, anyone's hand. The plant went extinct shortly after Isra'el capitulated to the Romans. Since that time, everyone assumed the persimmon plant to be forever gone.

Much to the surprise of everyone, in April, 1988, Professor Joseph Patrich of Hebrew and Haifa Universities made a remarkable discovery. As head of an archeological team excavating around the area where the Copper Scroll was found in what is today Jordan, and an extremely hot region of the Negev desert, he discovered a five-inch-diameter flask of the long lost anointing oil. Remarkably, the intact flask still contains about three cubic inches of oil that has been buried three feet deep for close to two thousand years.

Several months of exhaustive chemical analysis confirmed that the oil was extracted from the ancient persimmon plant. The Holy Oil had evidently been slipped out of the Temple by the High Priest just before or during the destruction of the Temple by the Romans and hidden along with the Copper Scroll.

What made the find even more exciting was the fact that the Holy Oil was still "a living" oil. Scientific chemical tests of the oil indicated that the oil was 19 centuries old and had survived in an incredibly good state of preservation. Everyone was amazed. The oil even reacted as the ancient texts said it would. When one drop of the oil was placed into water, the water became milky white.

Though there are no clear records from the period, Professor Patrich reiterated accounts of rabbis who described how the ancient persimmon oil—known as balsam oil to the Greeks of the time—had been poured over the heads of the ancient kings of Judah as part of the ceremony surrounding their ascension to the throne. The kingdom of Judah, comprising the southern tribes of the biblical Hebrews, lasted from 935 B.C.E. to 586 B.C.E. To quote from *A song of ascents,* a Psalm by David:

> Oh, how good, how pleasant it is for brothers to live together in harmony. It is like fragrant oil on the head that runs down over the beard, over the beard of Aharon, and flows down on the collar of his robes. It is like the dew of Hermon that settles on the mountains of Tziyon. For it was there that Adonai ordained the blessing of everlasting life.
> -- Psalm 133 (CJB)

Now we have truly sanctified oil as directed by Adonai to anoint Mashiach when he ascends to His throne.

Another problem or quandary surrounding Mashiach has been the ongoing debate among Jewish scholars regarding the concept of whether there are *two* appearances of *one* Mashiach, or whether Mashiach will be *two* people who will appear once or twice. Both Jews and Christian Bible critics claim the Tanakh says nothing about a Mashiach who will come twice as

Mashiach

indicated in the Christian Bible. Most Jews today hold to the idea that there is only one Mashiach who is yet to come; while a few, including Messianic Jews believe the major prophesies will only be fulfilled in a second coming of Mashiach who has *already* appeared once.

Historically there have been two different schools of thought by the rabbis of old regarding the appearance of the Anointed One. Several predicted the appearance of what is known as the *Suffering Servant* who will die for the sins of everyone, while the other school foretold that a Mashiach will come who will *Reign and Rule* over the entire world. It is most interesting to note that until the tenth century C.E., our Jewish religion had no fixed or rigid dogmas. Even our most devout teachers used the greatest freedom when discussing the concept of Mashiach.

One of the greatest of all prophecies in the Tanakh concerning the advent of Mashiach is found in the book of Isaiah, Chapters 52 and 53. This section of the Prophetic books, also known as the Suffering Servant prophecies, has been long understood by the historical Rabbis of Judaism to speak of the Redeemer who will one day come to Zion. Unfortunately, many modern Rabbis believe the Suffering Servant of Isaiah 53 refers to Isra'el, or to Isaiah himself, or even Moses, or another of the Jewish prophets. But Isaiah is clear. Isaiah speaks of Mashiach, as many ancient rabbis concluded.

Mashiach is also vividly pictured as the *Reign and Rule* king over the enemies of G-d. This will be a time of peace and joy! Isra'el will be the leader of all nations again, and the Davidic throne will once again re-establish in Jerusalem. As an example in Psalm 2:2-4 (CJB):

> The earth's kings are taking positions, leaders conspiring together, against Adonai and his anointed. They cry, "Let's break their fetters! Let's throw off their chains!" He who sits in heaven laughs; Adonai looks at them in derision.

And again in Jeremiah 23:5 (CJB):

> 'The days are coming,' says Adonai when I will raise a righteous Branch for David. He will reign as king and succeed; he will do what is just and right in the land.

There are many other Tanakh sources depicting a Reign and Rule King. "The scepter will not pass from Y'hudah, nor the ruler's staff from between his legs, until he comes to whom [obedience] belongs; and it is he whom the peoples will obey" (Genesis 49:10). The words, "scepter," and, "ruler's staff," show one reigning king. In Numbers 24:17, this king is prophesied again: "I see him, but not now; I behold him, but not soon—a star will step forth from Ya'akov, a scepter will arise from Isra'el." David prophesies to the extent and longevity of G-d's reign: "Your throne, G-d, will last forever and ever; you rule your kingdom with a scepter of equity" (Psalm 45:6-7). The King will

Mashiach

have a purpose. "He will judge between the nations and arbitrate for many peoples" (Isaiah 2:1-4).

He will come majestic, and everyone will see Him and know his power. "Come into the rock, hide in the dust to escape the terror of *Adonai* and the glory of his majesty" (Isaiah 11:10). He will have the capability to defeat enemies and alter the very fabric of our planet. "On that day his feet will stand on the Mount of Olives, which lies to the east of Yerushalayim; and the Mount of Olives will be split in half from east to west, to make a huge valley" (Zechariah 14:3-4). No credible writer denies these schools of thought predicting Mashiach. Yet what puzzles many today is how a single person can be both the *Suffering Servant* and the *Reign and Rule* King of the world in a single lifetime.

Examining the prophecies concerning the ruling and reigning Mashiach makes it clear his reign will last forever and ever. The obvious meaning of this particular line of prophecy shows us that his rule will have no ending; however, his rule does have a beginning! Which means that if this line of prophecy is to be fulfilled in the life of a single individual, one who will also be the *Suffering Servant*, then be rejected and die, then His everlasting triumph must logically be fulfilled last. It is logically impossible that the ruling and reigning prophecies would be fulfilled first, only to be interrupted by the rejection, suffering, and death of the individual. This would nullify the prophetic theme that the ruling and reigning would be forever and ever and ever … .

It appears as though the sages of old were

confused; and in order to solve the disagreement, the ancient rabbis created the "two Mashiach" idea in the first century C.E. (possibly the early second century C.E.). It can't be said who actually initiated this idea, but it became a fixture in Jewish law when rabbis of the day decided to split Mashiach into two—one for each line of prophecy. Two images of Mashiach which have led to numerous oral traditions foretelling **two** Mashiachs: Mashiach ben Yosef identified with the *Suffering Servant*, and Mashiach ben David identified with the *Reign and Rule* King. The latter would be a great military leader who is destined to re-build the Temple and protect and deliver Isra'el from its enemies.

No matter if you are interested in the suffering servant Mashiach or are looking at the rule and reign Mashiach, there is NOT a single occasion in the literature or the Messianic prophecies in the entire Tanakh where a **plural** pronoun was used.

Another school of reasoning is re-emerging in Jewish thought. It states that a single person can fulfill the two lines prophesied. However, as obvious logic dictates he would have to come *twice* which is currently a premise not generally accepted in Judaic circles. Still, did our early first-century ancestors and rabbis believe in this premise?

To repeat the quote above from Deuteronomy 18:15, 18-19 again, we read that G-d is going to "raise up a prophet" from among the Jewish people. This is stated twice, in verse 15 and again in verse 18.

Adonai will **raise up** for you a prophet like me

Mashiach

from among yourselves, from your own kinsmen. You are to pay attention to him, just as when you were assembled at Horev and requested Adonai your G-d, 'Don't let me hear the voice of Adonai my G-d any more, or let me see this great fire ever again; if I do, I will die!' On that occasion Adonai said to me, 'They are right in what they are saying. I will **raise up** for them a prophet like you from among their kinsmen. I will put my words in his mouth, and he will tell them everything I order him. Whoever doesn't listen to my words, which he will speak in my name, will have to account for himself to me.'
-- Deuteronomy 18:15-19 (CJB)

The Torah clearly states that Mashiach will become the greatest prophet in history, at least as great as Moses. The Spirit of Adonai will rest upon him. Mashiach will be in our world and also in full union with Adonai as shown in Isaiah 11:1-4 (CJB):

But a branch will emerge from the trunk of Yishai, a shoot will grow from his roots. The Spirit of Adonai will rest on him, the Spirit of wisdom and understanding, the Spirit of counsel and power, the Spirit of knowledge and fearing Adonai.

He will be inspired by fearing Adonai. He will not judge by what his eyes see or decide by what his ears hear, but he will judge the impoverished justly; he will decide fairly for the humble of the land…

Yet some skeptics state that it is impossible for G-d to send a true prophet in modern times, or even ancient times if it was after approximately 400 B.C.E. These skeptics go on to state that prophecy can only exist in Isra'el when the land is inhabited by a majority of world Jewry, a situation which has not existed since 300 BCE. During the time of Ezra when the majority of Jews remained in Babylon, prophecy ended upon the death of the last prophets Haggai, Zechariah and Malachi.

Was it through the prophet Malachi that G-d delivered His FINAL prophetic message to Jews? While there are other numerous examples which could be cited from Jewish history that contradict this premise, one example stands out as a major indication that prophecies did not stop even long after our prophet Malachi made his last revelation. That one good example is our story of Chanukkah, the Feast of Rededication.

G-d manifested Himself to guide the Maccabees through many battles which eventually gave them the ability to retake control of Jerusalem and the Holy Temple. G-d's message was clear. He would not allow the eradication of His people at that time in history, and He wanted them to continue the sacrificial system that had been instituted by Mosaic Law. While the joyous festival of Chanukkah may not be one of the most

Mashiach

important Jewish holidays and celebrations, today it ranks—along with Passover and Purim—as one of the most beloved Jewish family holidays.

Bottom line, prophecies continue until the present time, and people who maintain that prophets cannot appear in this world cannot be believed since the Scriptures do not say so. Thus any such statement should be considered pure blasphemy as it denigrates the power of G-d to do what He promised at a time of His own will and choosing. There is no place in the Tanakh that actually states that there will not be another Prophet after 300 B.C.E., or that prophecy ended upon the deaths of Haggai, Zechariah, and Malachi. These statements are pure human creation and frankly, self-serving opinion.

One group of devout people waiting during that early era for Mashiach was the Jewish movement called the Essenes. The Essenes were similar to the Pharisees in that they were strictly Torah observant. However they were also Messianic, apocalyptic, baptist (a washing ritual practiced by the Essenes that required a change of heart) wilderness, New Covenant Jewish sect. They were led by a priest they called the "Teacher of Righteousness." The movement formed during the Maccabean conflict around 160 B.C.E.

The Essenes believed that the Temple priests in Jerusalem were corrupt and the Temple was in need of serious reform. In their view, the coming of Mashiach was near. They believed He would join with them to throw off the oppressive yoke of Rome. During the years after the prophet Malachi, the Jewish world witnessed events that prepared the world for the coming of Mashiach. This period in history had a remarkable production of religious literature, including the translation of the Hebrew Bible into Greek and the beginning of the Essenes' creation of the Dead Sea Scrolls.

G-d promised to give us a New Covenant in Jeremiah 31:31 (CJB):

> It will not be like the covenant I made with their fathers on the day I took them by their hand and brought them out of the land of Egypt; because they, for their part, violated my covenant, even though I, for my part, was a husband to them, says Adonai.

Thus, if you believe in the accuracy of the Tanakh, you must believe that G-d did not finish communicating to His people upon the death of Malachi.

The Dead Sea Scrolls provide another area for discussion on later prophecy. The discussion in the scrolls generally focuses on what first century Jews thought about, and how they accepted ancient prophecy in their community. There are few books and studies about ongoing prophetic activity, which has primarily been because of the nature of the evidence in the scrolls themselves.

Let's turn now to a discussion of the Dead Sea Scrolls to examine how they relate to, and contain information about, Mashiach.

As we are all aware, in the spring of 1947 on the

Mashiach

western shore of the Dead Sea roughly eight miles south of Jericho, a young Bedouin shepherd climbed into a cave high up on a hillside in the Judean desert and stumbled upon a clay jar in a cave near Khirbet Qumran that contained seven parchment scrolls, *The Dead Sea Scrolls*. News of this extraordinary find spread from both Isra'eli and American sources rapidly. Seventy years of intense research into these Qumran texts has followed. Of these major studies and discoveries of what can be considered one of the greatest finds, were two complete copies of Isaiah, including an unbroken complete scroll of the book of Isaiah, 24 feet long, dating to around 200 B.C.E.

The 24-foot-long scroll is one thousand years older than the Masoretic text, the oldest known copy dating to 900 C.E. The late Gleason Archer examined these two Isaiah scrolls found in Cave 1 and wrote:

> Even though the two copies of Isaiah discovered in Qumran Cave 1 near the Dead Sea in 1947 were a thousand years earlier than the oldest dated manuscript previously known (A.D. 980), they proved to be **word for word identical** with our standard Hebrew Bible in more than 95 percent of the text. The five percent of variation consisted chiefly of obvious slips of the pen and variations in spelling.

The discovery of the Dead Sea Scrolls provides valuable evidence that the Tanakh had been accurately and carefully preserved and certainly provided proof of the discipline of the scribes over the centuries who were responsible for the hand copied Scriptures of Isaiah.

An article in *Biblical Archaeology Review* from 1992 has a compelling discussion of Qumran text 4Q521 in which the two author's discuss their findings from these ancient scrolls. They indicate a single Mashiach is coming. Their findings regarding the Essenes of Qumran declare Mashiach to be descended from King David and called him, "the teacher of righteousness." To quote these two Dead Sea Scroll scholars:

> Our Qumran text, 4Q521, is, astonishingly, quite close to this Christian concept of the Mashiach. Our text speaks not only of a single Messianic figure...but it also describes him in extremely exalted terms, as a cosmic agent.
>
> That there was, in fact, an expectation of a single Messianic figure at Qumran is really not so surprising. A reexamination of the Qumran literature on this subject leads one to question the two Mashiach theory. As a matter of fact, only once in any Dead Sea Scroll text is the idea of two Mashiachs stated unambiguously.
> -- Michael Wise and James Tabor

These Jewish scholars were convinced that the Essenes applied both lines of prophecy to a single Mashiach. According to Wise and Tabor, the Qumran

Mashiach

community believed Mashiach would come once and "suffer initial defeat;" and later he would "triumph in the end of days." Two appearances of a single Mashiach! One appearance in humility and one in glory!

G-d's plan for Isra'el demands the appearance of Mashiach. Our G-d who made known His laws through Moses to Isra'el and instructed us to keep them will establish his rule physically on earth in Isra'el. Yet we have seen many kingdoms come and pass before the Kingdom of G-d. Quoting the Midrash of the Ten Kings, Samuel S. Cohon, in his "Divine Kingship in the Bible" as follows:

> The first kingdom was that of the King of Kings, the L-rd of Hosts. There followed the kingdom of Nimrod, Pharaoh, Isra'el, Nebuchadnezzar, Ahasuerus, Greece and Rome. The ninth kingdom will be that of the Mashiach of the house of David, and the tenth will be again that of the King of Kings and L-rd of Hosts--may it soon be revealed to us and to all the inhabitants of earth.

The prophet Zechariah also anticipates the arrival of Mashiach and the ninth kingdom:

> I will pour out on the house of David and on those living in Yerushalayim a spirit of grace and prayer; and they will look to me, whom they pierced. They will mourn for him as one

mourns for an only son; they will be in bitterness on his behalf like the bitterness for a firstborn son.

When that day comes, there will be great mourning in Yerushalayim, mourning like that for Hadad-Rimmon in the Megiddo Valley. Then the land will mourn, each family by itself — the family of the house of David by itself, and their wives by themselves; the family of the house of Natan by itself, and their wives by themselves; the family of the house of Levi by itself, and their wives by themselves; the family of the Shim'i by itself, and their wives by themselves; all the remaining families, each by itself, and their wives by themselves.

-- Zechariah 12:10-14 (CJB)

Does Mashiach come only once and triumphantly establish his throne and new Kingdom in Jerusalem?

Are there really two Mashiachs, the *Suffering Servant* who would die for the sins of everyone, followed by another Mashiach who will come and *Reign and Rule* the world?

Or are the Qumran scholars right? There is only one Mashiach who comes once, "suffers initial defeat," and then at a later time "ultimately triumphs in the end of days." Two appearances of a *single* Mashiach! One appearance in humility and one in glory!

Scripture provides a picture of a returning King: "I will go and return to my place, till they admit their guilt

Mashiach

and search for me, seeking me eagerly in their distress" (Hosea 5:15).

Going back to the opening sentence of this Chapter: "Who" is Mashiach? Throughout today's Talmud and Tanakh translations, there does not appear an actual name for Mashiach. However, if one goes back to earlier versions of the Talmud, there are a few references that mention the name Yeshua.

Uncensored texts of the Babylonian Talmud and the Tosefta discuss the name, Yeshua. In the first few centuries C.E., history indicates there were many sects of Judaism: from the Pharisees, Sadducees, and Essenes, to the Herodians, Zealots, High Priests, Scribes, and the original Messianic Jews. The latter were referred to as Early Christians, or Judeo-Christians, each of these sects claimed their religion was the correct faith. However, according to Josephus, the famous first-century historian, only three of these were accepted as major forms of Jewish philosophy being pursued by the Judeans: the Pharisees, the Sadducees, and the Essenes

In modern twentieth and twenty-first century literature, there are important Jewish writers who mention Yeshua. In 1922 Joseph Klausner wrote, *Yeshu ha-Notzri* ("Jesus of Nazareth") which concludes: "...the evidence [for a historical Yeshua] in the Talmud is scanty and does not contribute much to our knowledge of the historical Yeshua is merely legendary." However, he concludes that some historic material about Yeshua *is* reliable.

In 2007, Peter Schäfer wrote, *Jesus in the Talmud,*

in which he tries to find a middle ground between "anti-Jewish Christian" and "apologetic Jewish" interpretations. He concludes that the references to Yeshua as the Messiah of Christianity had been included in the early 3rd and 4th century versions of the Talmud.

Another dispute in Judaism regards the question of the Christians belief that Mashiach is a physical incarnation of G-d and part of a Triune G-d. A complete study of the G-dhead is an enormous task. A study of the Triune nature of G-d or the divinity of Yeshua while difficult to comprehend is a necessary task if we want to understand Mashiach. To orthodox Jews as well as some conservative Jews, the idea of G-d becoming a man is just an impossibility that goes against Judaism's strict monotheism. Hence, G-d is non-tangible and certainly not part human and that settles it! A considerable number of Jews today assume the entire belief in the deity of Yeshua is merely a Christian invention that developed much later in church history. Hence, the Christian theological concepts like the incarnation, the virgin birth, and the Trinity, are totally foreign to both Judaism and the Tanakh.

While it is universally believed by both Jews and Christians that G-d is One, and that there is no one beside Him, the tri-unity of G-d is clearly taught in the Torah and throughout the Tanakh books. Not only in the Bible but also in the Talmudical & Rabbinical writings are a Triune G-d concept well-known and affirmed. Space does not permit listing of all the sources, but a few of them are as follows.

Mashiach

In the Torah, when G-d (Elohim) creates the universe and the Earth within it, He wants to make it abundantly clear to mankind that He is not like some abstract principle. That is evident in Genesis 1:

> Then G-d said, "Let **us** make humankind in **our** image, in the likeness of **ourselves**; and let them rule over the fish in the sea, the birds in the air, the animals, and over all the earth, and over every crawling creature that crawls on the earth." -- Genesis 1:26 (CJB)

What G-d clearly states is that He created man in the image of G-d, who is a triunity, with a body, soul and spirit. He reveals Himself in the plural form of **Elohim**. Deuteronomy 10:17 states: *"For Adonai your G-d is G-d of gods."* El means *mighty* or *strong* and is used in the Torah for reference to gods, including Almighty G-d. Elohim is the main word translated from Hebrew in the Torah. The *him* ending of Elohim translated from Hebrew is the plural ending, meaning *more than one*. Elohim is even used in Genesis 1:1 as G-d as Creator: "In the beginning G-d created the heavens and the earth." This could just as easily be translated: "In the beginning **G-ds** created the heavens and the earth."

In Genesis 1:2, YHWH says: "The earth was unformed and void, darkness was on the face of the deep, and the Spirit of G-d (Ruach) hovered over the surface of the water." In speaking of where "the Spirit of G-d (Ruach) hovered," some translations say, "brooded upon the face of the water." It is interesting to note that early Rabbinic commentary (Bereshis Rabba 2) says that "Ruach" is the Spirit of King Mashiach.

Notwithstanding today's Jewish beliefs, most knowledgeable rabbi—even though they don't accept the triunity of G-d—admit that this quotation in Genesis supports the concept of a triune G-d.

In Midrash Rabbah, these comments are found on Genesis 1:26:

> Rabbi Samuel bar Nahman in the name of Rabbi Jonathan said, that at the time when Moses wrote the Torah; writing a portion of it daily, when he came to this Verse which says, 'And Elohim said let **us** make man in **our** image after **our** likeness,' Moses said, Master of the Universe why do you give herewith an excuse to the sectarians   (who believe in the triunity of G-d). G-d answered Moses, '**You write and whoever wants to err let him err.**'

G-d was writing directly through Moses, not to have everyone make a mistake but to reveal to each of us His nature. He is a triune G-d who tells us He is Elohim.

Through the Prophets, He describes Himself as "The Word" through which he created everything. He also reveals Himself as the Ruakh Hakodesh, or Holy Spirit, who was the inspiration of the prophets of G-d and who showed great miracles through the judges of Isra'el, David, Samson, Gideon, and the "Son" in

Mashiach

David's book of Psalms.

In the book of Isaiah the prophet speaks in the name of G-d:

> Come close to me, and listen to this: since the beginning I have not spoken in secret, since the time things began to be, I have been there; and now Adonai Elohim has sent me and his Spirit.   -- Isaiah 48:16 (CJB)

G-d wanted all His people to come to Him. To enable humanity to understand Him, the L-rd G-d sent His Spirit. These are the identical teachings as we find in the Torah. Just as He directed Moses to show his triunitarian nature, He also spoke through the Prophets of Isra'el to do so also.

This same Holy Spirit was very clearly speaking through David and telling him that Jehovah has a Son begotten of G-d in a supernatural manner:

> I will proclaim the decree: Adonai said to me,
> You are my **son**; today I became your father.
>   -- Psalm 2:7 (CJB)

And then again later in chapter two of the Psalms:

> Serve Adonai with fear; rejoice, but with trembling. Kiss the **son**, lest he be angry, and you perish along the way, when suddenly his anger blazes. How blessed are all who take refuge in him.   -- Psalm 2:11-12 (CJB)

D.A. Osterman

Most Jews have been brought up to think that if we believe that G-d is One, then this idea excludes any idea of G-d manifesting Himself as the Son or as the Ruakh Hakodesh, or Holy Spirit. A concept of a triune G-d's seemed to be a pagan idea.

With all this in mind, let's look at the Tanakh and its many prophesies to see what it says concerning Mashiach as we examine the six Jewish traditions that surround him.

Mashiach

Chapter 4
The "Kingdom of G-d" and
Creating a Worldwide Reign of Peace

The first tradition states that the Mashiach will bring universal disarmament and worldwide reign of peace with a complete end to war (Micah 4:1-4; Hoseah 2:20; Isaiah 2:1-4, 60:18). Examining these scriptures proves we are called to the promised hope of the Prophets in the Tanakh. We Jews have an eternal inheritance from G-d.

Clearly the Tanakh prophets portrayed a picture of Mashiach ruling and reigning while freeing Isra'el. Mashiach will end all war and will have all-inclusive knowledge of G-d.

> In the acharit-hayamim the mountain of Adonai's house will be established as the most important mountain. It will be regarded more highly than the other hills, and all the Goyim will stream there.   -- Isaiah 2:1-4 (CJB).

37

In the prophet Isaiah's book, we learn of His arrival as follows:

> On that day Adonai will raise his hand again, a second time, to reclaim the remnant of his people who remain from Ashur, Egypt, Patros, Ethiopia, 'Eilam, Shin'ar, Hamat and the islands in the sea.   -- Isaiah 11:11 (CJB)

Further prophesies of a Second Kingdom appear in Ezekiel 40-48, Daniel 2:44, Zechariah 14. At the same time, other prophecies speak of Mashiach suffering as atonement for sin. Psalm 22 talks of One "who can't keep himself alive" (verse 30). Isaiah further expounds on the Mashiach's atonement for our sins:

> See how my servant will succeed! He will be raised up, exalted, highly honored! Just as many were appalled at him, because he was so disfigured that he didn't even seem human and simply no longer looked like a man, so now he will startle many nations; because of him, kings will be speechless. For they will see what they had not been told, they will ponder things they had never heard.
> -- Isaiah 52:13-53:12 (CJB)

The passage clearly pertains to someone who will "startle" nations and kings. Humanity will be struck in awe, amazed, even stunned by Mashiach. Who can make people, nations, and kings speechless? And how can a person ponder "things" that are "never heard?" This must mean a spiritual manifestation on Earth—a supernatural occurrence—the Mashiach's arrival will shock everyone and alter our planet and humanity. An "anointed prince" will come (Daniel 9:25-26) and the days ahead will be planet altering and people changing:

> Adonai will save the tents of Y'hudah first, so that the glory of the house of David and the glory of those living in Yerushalayim will not appear greater than that of Y'hudah. When that day comes, Adonai will defend those living in Yerushalayim. On that day, even someone who stumbles will be like David; and the house of David will be like G-d, like the angel of Adonai before them. When that day comes, I will seek to destroy all nations attacking Yerushalayim; and I will pour out on the house of David and on those living in Yerushalayim a spirit of grace and prayer; and they will look to me, whom they pierced.
> -- Zechariah 12:10 (CJB)

Most noticeable in the above passage is the last phrase: "They will look to me, whom they pierced." This verse indicates a future time when the Jewish people will plead for the mercy of G-d. This will happen when they see "the one they already pierced." Interestingly, this correlates with the discussion in the Brit Chadasha when Yeshua, hanging on the cross, was pierced with a spear by a Roman soldier.

This prophecy about Mashiach obviously has not yet been fulfilled. However, Zechariah does foretell of a future time when all of Jerusalem will see Mashiach and mourn. At which time, they will cry out to G-d for mercy, and He will answer them by saving them from their enemies: "On that day the L-RD will shield those who live in Jerusalem. . . . I will set out to destroy all the nations that attack Jerusalem" (Zechariah 12:8-9). Mashiach will stop all wars after His arrival as Micah 4:3 (CJB) says:

> He will judge between many peoples and arbitrate for many nations far away. Then they will hammer their swords into plow-blades and their spears into pruning-knives; nations will not raise swords at each other, and they will no longer learn war.   -- Micah 4:3 (CJB)

Isaiah 2:4 contains a very similar passage as follows:

> He will judge between the nations and arbitrate for many peoples." Not only will there no longer be any war, but the weapons will be dismantled and battle strategies will no longer be taught.   -- Isaiah 2:4 (CJB)

Isra'el will enjoy peace and be completely safe in the kingdom:

Mashiach

The days are coming, says Adonai when I will raise a righteous Branch for David. He will reign as king and succeed; he will do what is just and right in the land. In his days Y'hudah will be saved, Isra'el will live in safety, and the name given to him will be Adonai Tzidkenu [Adonai our Righteousness].

-- Jeremiah 23:5-6 (CJB)

Obviously this is quite different when compared to today's Isra'el that is surrounded by the likes of the current regime of the Mullah's in Iran and the expanding ISIS/ISIL Islamic State in Iraq and Syria. The latter is attempting to create an Islamic caliphate and has a bloodthirsty vision for anyone not of Islam.

Yet, even though things may look really good or really bleak at times in our government affairs or daily lives, and whatever 'peak' or 'valley' we're going through personally, nothing will compare to what G-d has prepared for us. The prophets longed to see how and when Mashiach would be revealed, and G-d gave them glimpses of various attributes. One of them brings us to our question: "Will Mashiach restore the throne of David and set up the Kingdom of G-d?" The Davidic Covenant is where the foundation of the reign of Mashiach is grounded. It includes promises to David of Prosperity, a throne of royal authority, a Kingdom and rule on earth and fulfillment of the promises to David forever.

Many Judaic scholars have dedicated years to the study of the Kingdom. Countless books have been

41

written about the Kingdom of G-d. So this single chapter dedicated to the Kingdom cannot do it justice; but hopefully, it will be a good beginning for further personal study.

The term "Mashiach" is frequently restricted to an exact concept, the "anointed king" of the Davidic dynasty that would create the kingdom intended by G-d for Isra'el. In Judaism, the "Kingdom of G-d," or the "Kingdom of Heaven," is a Messianic term. It refers to a kingdom that Mashiach will establish. The definition most used is: the sovereignty of G-d as acknowledged by us humans.

As postulated in Chapter 2, the sages were obviously confused about how to interpret the two distinct pictures of Mashiach presented by the Tanakh prophets. On the one hand there is the "Reign and Rule" King who arrives regally on a cloud (Daniel 7:13) destined to triumph and deliver the Jews. On the other hand, there is the "Suffering Servant" who is born to meager parents, humbly rides into Jerusalem on a donkey (Zechariah 9:9), and who dies for the sins of everyone.

The Jewish reference book, *Concise Companion to the Jewish Religion*, reads: "It is the rabbinic expression for the sovereignty of G-d as acknowledged by human beings." It is broken down into three aspects as follows:

1. An individual accepts the yoke of the kingdom of heaven when he recites the Shema or Deuteronomy 6:4: 'Hear O Isra'el

Mashiach

the L-rd our G-d, the L-rd is one.'
2. Universally, it is the kingdom that Mashiach will establish over all peoples.
3. Nationalistically, it is when the people of Isra'el will be redeemed from subservience to earthly rulers.

The concept of the "Kingdom of G-d" is the realization of a series of prophecies over several centuries. Indeed, one of the most awe inspiring teachings in the Tanakh is the coming of King Mashiach to establish His everlasting Kingdom on earth stated in Ezekiel:

> He said, 'Human being, this is the place for my throne, the place for the soles of my feet, where I will live among the people of Isra'el forever. The house of Isra'el, both they and their kings, will never again defile my holy name by their prostitution, by [burying] the corpses of their kings [on] their high places.'
> -- Ezekiel 43:7 (CJB)

This "Davidic Covenant" was created when David was promised that one of his descendants would rule on his throne forever. In 2 Samuel 7:12-17, the prophecy is fulfilled in part as David's son Solomon takes the throne as follows:

> When your days come to an end and you sleep with your ancestors, I will establish one of

43

your descendants to succeed you, one of your own flesh and blood; and I will set up his rulership. He will build a house for my name, and I will establish his royal throne forever. I will be a father for him, and he will be a son for me. If he does something wrong, I will punish him with a rod and blows, just as everyone gets punished; nevertheless, my grace will not leave him, as I took it away from Sha'ul, whom I removed from before you. Thus your house and your kingdom will be made secure **forever** before you; your throne will be set up forever.

But the single word "forever" obviously indicates there are successors to come in his lineage.

Many of the scriptural requirements concerning Mashiach, what he will do, and what will be done during his reign are located in the Book of Isaiah. Isaiah is known by many as Mashiach prophet. The book is so full and rich in detail it is hard to write a synopsis. Since time before creation, G-d planned for himself a kingdom and home here on Earth. Indeed, in Isaiah 9:6-7 (CJB) G-d declares:

> ...in order to extend the dominion and perpetuate the peace of the throne and kingdom of David, to secure it and sustain it through justice and righteousness hence forth and forever. The zeal of Adonai-Tzva'ot will accomplish this. -- Isaiah 9:6-7 (CJB)

Mashiach

This long awaited era will be ushered in by Mashiach ("the Anointed One"), a virtuous descendant of King David. He will rebuild our Temple as well as bring the Jewish people from around the world, back to Isra'el.

Why is the coming of Mashiach a center-piece of the Jewish belief system? Why is this important today, two or three millennium after He was first prophesied? Because as we have learned from the Torah, we have a purpose in our lives and in our world. The truth of Jewish life today is the realization of this as an essential theme in our Judaic tradition.

The world is in critical need of Mashiach redemption. While in Judaism, there is no specific time prophesied when Mashiach comes. Instead, it is the actions (or lack of actions) of humanity that determines when Mashiach comes. It is said that Mashiach will come either when the world needs his coming the most (when the world is so sinful and in desperate need of saving by Mashiach) or deserves it the most (when genuine goodness prevails in the world).

To the extent that any of us are conscious of our yetzer hara side and repent for straying from the path of righteousness will show the degree to which we crave to be saved. As we see in the Talmud, at the seat of judgment every Jew will be required to answer the question: "Did you long for the coming of the Mashiach?"

Part of the prophecy of Mashiach's Kingdom is that while Mashiach reigns as King of Isra'el, the Jews will be ingathered from their exile and return to Isra'el, their homeland. In spite of the dire announcements in today's news almost daily, we seem to be getting closer to that time when we will be rescued by Mashiach. Indeed, a particularly bright spot on the world stage is this portion of the prophet's prediction that has to a great extent already been fulfilled. The Jewish people have returned to Isra'el and these early settlers have made the barren land to bloom again.

This re-birth of Isra'el is a promise from G-d fulfilled. That our people could be dispersed all over the world and survive as a people for over 1900 years, and then have David Ben-Gurion on May 14, 1948 proclaim the Jewish State of Isra'el must certainly be considered miraculous.

No one knows when Mashiach will come, but as King David says in Psalms 95:7: "Redemption will come today—if you hearken to His voice." And as we saw in Isaiah 9:7 above, he speaks of a time when G-d would restore the Davidic dynasty ensuring its permanence, and emancipate the Jew's from alien rule.

Amos 9:11-15 states that Mashiach will emerge from the Davidic lineage that fulfills G-d's covenant promises:

> When that day comes, I will raise up the fallen sukkah of David. I will close up its gaps, raise up its ruins and rebuild it as it used to be, so that Isra'el can possess what is left of Edom and of all the nations bearing my name, says Adonai, who is doing this. The days will

come, says Adonai, when the plowman will overtake the reaper and the one treading grapes the one sowing seed. Sweet wine will drip down the mountains, and all the hills will flow with it. I will restore the fortunes of my people Isra'el; they will rebuild and inhabit the ruined cities; they will plant vineyards and drink their wine, cultivate gardens and eat their fruit. I will plant them on their own soil, no more to be uprooted from their land, which I gave them, says Adonai your G-d.

Ezekiel declares a new David will be a shepherd as well as a "prince" and a "King" to Isra'el.

I will raise up one shepherd [king] to be in charge of them, and he will let them feed — my servant David. He will pasture them and be their shepherd. I, Adonai, will be their G-d; and my servant David will be prince among them. I, Adonai, have spoken.
-- Ezekiel 34:23-24 (CJB)

The promises yet unfilled which were given to Isra'el in the Tanakh serve as an outline of the plan G-d has for his people. While to many these promises seem to be on hold—and it is clear that many of them are yet unfulfilled—we need to trust that G-d has had a plan for us since before He created the earth. Ultimately, we know from scripture that G-d will not only restore Isra'el to a place of blessing, but also fulfill the land

and Kingdom promises made to his people.

It is clear that during G-d's reign from Isra'el after the arrival of Mashiach, all of the Davidic covenants will be fulfilled. Isra'el will be in her glory, and the rest of the earth will be given great blessings as well. Everyone will be given responsibilities that will focus on Mashiach as he will be in our presence as he "Reigns and Rules" from Isra'el.

The fulfillment of the Davidic covenant certainly has not happened, thus far. Yet as discussed in Chapter 2, the concept of a single Mashiach coming twice, has the most credibility when reading the Tanakh in its most literal sense accompanied by the wisdom of the rabbis of old and the ancient Qumran, "Dead Sea Scrolls." Mashiach will return to reign and rule the world from Isra'el.

Mashiach

Chapter 5
Rebuilding the Holy Temple

The second tradition states that the Temple in Jerusalem will be rebuilt. Isaiah 2:2-3 states:

In the acharit-hayamim the mountain of Adonai's house will be established as the most important mountain. It will be regarded more highly than the other hills, and all the Goyim will stream there. Many peoples will go and say, "Come, let's go up to the mountain of Adonai, to the house of the G-d of Ya'akov! He will teach us about his ways, and we will walk in his paths." For out of Tziyon will go forth Torah, the word of Adonai from Yerushalayim.

Other passages prophesying a third Temple can be found in Isaiah 56:6-7, Isaiah 60:7, Isaiah 66:20, Ezekiel 37:26–27, Malachi 3:4, and Zechariah 14:20-21.

This tradition also raises another question. Will the Holy Temple in Jerusalem be rebuilt before the

D.A. Osterman

appearance of Mashiach, or after his arrival? Only a small number of Orthodox Jewish believers in Isra'el today believe that the coming Third Temple will be built by Mashiach when he appears. The current thinking among biblical scholars, including those representing the ultra-Orthodox Temple Institute, believe they need to make all possible preparations in advance to build the Third Temple as soon as it is possible politically without creating an outright war with today's Muslim community. Whether Mashiach arrives before or after a Third Temple is erected is irrelevant as far as they are concerned.

There are at least three reasons we can expect a new Temple to be rebuilt in Jerusalem in contemporary times before the arrival of Mashiach. Firstly, all Jews agree that we want one. Secondly, the Tanakh declares that it WILL be constructed. Thirdly, modern rabbinical scholars teach that the Temple and everything it represents could be rebuilt even today. These scholars of Judaism, and scholars of our 1,900-year-long, post Temple era say the Third Temple is already constructed in heaven as G-d waits for us Jews to complete all the groundwork we need to finish it here on Earth. G-d is ready when we are!

The fact that the Third Temple could be built at any time is easily shown in the Tanakh. However, before we embark on any construction of a new Temple, we must look to the Talmud and understand why the old Temple was destroyed. Learning from out past sins and mistakes helps ensure we don't repeat them.

Mashiach

The moral of a story from the Talmud (Gittin 56) explains why the old Temple was destroyed. Because of the hatred of one Jew against another Jew, G-d withdrew his spiritual force from the Temple. This led to the Siege of Jerusalem in 70 C.E., which was the decisive event of the first Jewish–Roman War. The siege ended with the sacking of Jerusalem and the destruction of the famous Second Temple. Symbolically, this burning into ashes was merely the burning of a building already in a state of spiritual ashes. Thus, before we begin the reconstruction of a third Temple, we Jews must examine our hearts and motives, and pray that our G-d will cleanse us and make us worthy of his presence once again.

The restoration of the walls and Temple has been-and-is being protracted because of a clash between Palestinians and Isra'eli activists who want to abolish the current restrictions preventing Jews from praying at Temple Mount. A decade's long peace agreement has been challenged almost from the day the government imposed restrictions on Jewish prayer there, after the 1967 Middle East war when Isra'el seized control of east Jerusalem.

Tensions in Isra'el during the fall of 2014 were rising over the Jerusalem shrine, known to Muslims as Haram as-Sharif (or Noble Sanctuary) and to Jews as the Temple Mount. However, Isra'eli government spokesman Mark Regev quoted Prime Minister Benjamin Netanyahu as telling security officials, "There will be no change in the status quo at the Temple Mount." Moshe Feiglin, a lawmaker from

Netanyahu's Likud Party, said that the struggle there was directly related to Isra'eli efforts to achieve overall security throughout the country, and that: "Any pullback from the Temple Mount will not end just at its gates. This society has to decide whether it is willing to pay the price to maintain its control, not only at the site, but in Isra'el as a whole."

How and when Isra'el will progress with the development of the Third Temple certainly is not clear. Even rabbinical opinion over prayer at the sacred site is deeply divided. Many ultra-Orthodox rabbis oppose prayer there under current conditions as a sacrilege.

Once seen as a symbol of Jerusalem unity that Isra'eli officials have long sought to project, the Temple is now becoming an increasing focus of the city's opposing political tensions.

The current attitude of the Isra'eli people and their leaders shows there is no desire to build the third temple right now. Today's Isra'eli citizens are very secular. Knowing full well that any attempt to build a third temple would result in immediate war with the Muslims, which with the ISIL Muslim radicals only a few miles away, this is a very serious threat.

In spite of this fear, our ultra-Orthodox brothers as mentioned in the opening paragraph to this chapter have a passion for The Third Temple. They are making and have made many of the required preparations. But the secular population is not willing today to support such a risky venture. Without a demand for a new temple, most Jewish observers believe a rally for a new temple must occur first. However, there has been considerable

Mashiach

preparation for the Third Temple!   According to a study undertaken by journalist and social activist Yizhar Beer in 2013 for the Ir Amim organization, twelve official groups are working in Isra'el today to establish the temple. A few receive funding in the range of hundreds of thousands of shekels annually from the Isra'eli government. One of these is the Temple Institute.

Recently this ultra-Orthodox Temple Institute announced they have completed the Tzitz, the High Priest's headplate. It is made of pure gold, was fashioned over a period of more than a year and is ready to be worn by the High Priest in the rebuilt Holy Third Temple in Jerusalem. The ultra-Orthodox Rabbi Richman a representative of the Temple Institute went on to say:

We have begun work on 120 sets of garments for 'regular' priests, not the High Priest. This involves special thread from India. In addition, we have begun work on architectural blueprints for the Third Temple, including cost projection, modern supplies, electricity, plumbing, and the computers needed to keep the temple organized and running efficiently and correctly.

We also know from various news reports that cedar from Lebanon captured in the north during the war there in 1982 has been placed in storage for the next temple. In addition the ultra-Orthodox movement, both the Ashkenazi and Sephardic Chief Rabbis of Jerusalem agree that such a temple will be built as soon as circumstances permit.

Secular Jews, while reluctant, don't believe a new

Third Temple should be built today. However, they do agree with their religious brothers and sisters, who are in distress and wondering, Are we all just dreaming, as Isra'el's leaders appear to be giving away the country in a futile attempt to find peace? Even though most of us are questioning what will happen next, Jewish presence on the Temple Mount is gaining ground in Jewish-Isra'eli discourse. Members of the Knesset and rabbis are ascending to the Temple Mount more frequently, and a surprising thirty percent of all Isra'elis' surveyed, as reported by Haaretz digital, on July 12, 2013, are calling for the construction of the Third Temple. But that still leaves seventy percent with an overall negative attitude.

Will our current leaders allow the ultra-Orthodox movement to commence with their desires? Or will they end up giving away our Jerusalem, our Temple Mount, and other national assets? Only G-d knows what the future holds for our Temple.

Current day tensions aside, G-d's truths concerning our third Temple appear in the Tanakh. Maimonides has stated it is incumbent on us to keep the temple in Jerusalem. The Third Temple must be placed on the same spot of ground as the First and Second Temples to obey our concept of "G-d's zones of holiness" on YHWH's sacred mountain.

However, differing groups of very astute modern-day researchers and archeologists disagree on the exact location. Some, including renowned Jerusalem archaeologist, Dan Bahat, say that both the First and Second Temples were located where the "Dome of the

Mashiach

Rock" resides today. Another group led by Dr. Asher Kaufman, formerly of the prestigious Racah Institute of Physics at Hebrew University, claims the location is actually just north of the Dome of the Rock on what is known as the paved platform area. A third view asserted by Architect Tuvia Sagiv situates the Temple south of the Dome. Wherever we decide to erect our Temple, we must beware of some of the frightening warnings in the Tanakh surrounding it.

The book of Daniel speaks of the future when "The Man of Sin," called the "ruler who will come" (Daniel 9:26). He will make a treaty with Isra'el to protect her for seven years, but then he will break the covenant in the middle of the treaty; and the Temple in Jerusalem will suffer ultimate defilement by a false Mashiach who claims to be G-d as indicated by the following verses:

> Alliances will be made with him, but he will undermine them by deceit. Then, although he will have but a small following, he will emerge and become strong. Without warning, he will assail the most powerful men in each province and do things his predecessors never did, either recently or in the distant past; he will reward them with plunder, spoil and wealth while devising plots against their strongholds, but only for a time.
> -- Daniel 11:24-25 (CJB)

Because ships from Kittim [a settlement in present-day Larnaca on the west coast of

> Cyprus] will come against him, so that his
> courage will fail him. Then, in retreat, he will
> take furious action against the holy covenant,
> again showing favor to those who abandon the
> holy covenant.   -- Daniel 11:30 (CJB)

However, since only a properly consecrated Temple can
be defiled, Daniel shows that there will be a dedicated
"Third Temple" and priesthood at the time Mashiach
appears.

The coming false Jewish Mashiach will resemble
his predecessor Antiochus Epiphanes, the "worthless
shepherd," spoken about by Zechariah. Most Tanakh
scholars today are in agreement that the aharit ha-
yamim (End Time) tribulation period described in
Daniel's "Seventieth Week" encompasses just seven
years during which time the Third Temple will be
destroyed once again. The false Mashiach will let the
temple remain consecrated for a short period of time,
most estimates suggest just three-and-a-half years,
before he defiles the Holy place for the last three-and-a-
half years. During the latter, the Temple will be
desecrated by this "False Mashiach" in what Daniel
calls the "Abomination of Desolation." The False
Mashiach sets up an idol of himself in the great Third
Temple as Daniel describes:

> The king will do as he pleases. He will exalt
> himself and consider himself greater than any
> god, and he will utter monstrous blasphemies
> against the G-d of gods. He will prosper only

Mashiach

until the period of wrath is over, for what has been determined must take place.
                                                -- Daniel 11:36 (CJB)

However, the Third Temple will have a limited lifetime and use. It may be destroyed either in a time of war to come, or in the "great earthquake described by Ezekiel as shaking the land of Isra'el just prior to the coming of Mashiach. When the false Mashiach desecrates the Temple the true Mashiach will appear as prophesied in Ezekiel:

In my jealousy, in my heated fury I speak: when that day comes there will be a great earthquake in the land of Isra'el.
                                                -- Ezekiel 38:19 (CJB)

And again in Isaiah:

But your many foes will become like fine powder, the horde of tyrants like blowing chaff, and it will happen very suddenly. You will be visited by Adonai-Tzva'ot with thunder, earthquakes and loud noises, whirlwinds, tempests, flaming firestorms. Then, all the nations fighting Ari'el, everyone at war with her, the ramparts around her, the people that trouble her will fade like a dream, like a vision in the night.
                                                -- Isaiah 29:5-7 (CJB)

This brings us back to the question as to precisely when the third temple will be rebuilt.

The Tanakh does not reveal the answer to this question. All it says for certain is that the temple will be in existence before the false Mashiach reveals himself. Since this will be for only a short number of years, most scholars have concluded that the third Temple will likely be rebuilt before the period of the false Mashiach begins.

Today, some are saying that a Temple could be erected literally overnight, using a tent, like the Tabernacle of Moses. The Temple Institute is prepared to do this at a moment's notice! This would allow for the resumption of sacrifices while construction of the grand structure of the "Third Temple" commenced around and over the temporary Tabernacle tent. Furthermore, the possibility exists that the great Third Temple will be erected in a location next to the Al-Aqsa Mosque, the "Dome of the Rock." However, current architectural designs would impose restrictions on those locations. Yet many people are convinced the Isra'eli government WILL agree with the construction of the Third Holy Temple. In spite of personal opinions and convictions, everyone understands that those who are committed to establishing the Temple are logical and reasonable. There isn't going to be any work allowed in the Temple Mount area capable of jeopardizing the security and safety of Isra'el and G-d's people. When the time is right, the government will support the drive for a temple and make it happen. Just as the Jewish people under the leadership of David Ben-Gurion

Mashiach

established the State of Isra'el on May 14, 1948, we will someday agree to build the Third Holy Temple in an orderly, Isra'eli-government authorized process.

Whether the Third Holy Temple will be built where the Muslim Dome is currently, or somewhere north or south of the Dome, scholars and ultra-Orthodox of today will need to sort out which location is the actual spot where Solomon's Temple and the second Herod Temple "Holy of Holies" was located. Reading from the Prophets and looking at what is happening in the news today, many believe this will happen in the near future. There is a distinct possibility that this magnificent Third Holy Temple will actually be destroyed again. No one knows for sure, but it is easy to imagine that Mashiach himself could destroy the Third Temple as a result of the desecration by the false Mashiach. Worse yet, a horrendous (most likely nuclear) war would not only destroy the temple, but also the entire city of Jerusalem, killing millions of Isra'eli citizens. The Prophet Zechariah predicted this war. 2500 years ago he described a nuclear explosion in the only words he could possibly understand as follows:

> Their flesh rots away while they are standing on their feet, their eyes rot away in their sockets, and their tongues rot away in their mouths.   -- Zechariah 14:12 (CJB)

Will Mashiach himself construct a Holy Temple? With the distinct possibility that the third temple will be destroyed, there is another concept emerging which is controversial to some but quite real for others. If the Third Temple is destroyed then a fourth Temple prophesied by Zechariah (ca. 500 B.C.E.) describes Mashiach, whom he calls the "Sprout" or "Branch," will build a temple in Isra'el as the following scripture states:

> Take silver and gold; make crowns; put one on the head of Y'hoshua the son of Y'hotzadak, the cohen hagadol; and tell him, 'Adonai-Tzva'ot says: "There is coming a man whose name is Tzemach [Sprout]. He will sprout up from his place and rebuild the temple of Adonai. Yes, he will rebuild the temple of Adonai; and he will take up royal splendor, sitting and ruling from his throne. There will be a cohen before his throne; and they will accept each other's advice in complete harmony.   -- Zechariah 6:11-13 (CJB)

The prophet Ezekiel (Ezekiel 40-48) describes in great detail this new temple in Isra'el that is quite fascinating. It is so large that it is not possible for it to fit on the Temple Mount site. Using a literal reading of the Tanakh and assuming a physical appearance of Mashiach, there may yet be a Fourth Temple built which will be undertaken by Mashiach himself. Ezekiel's temple is also very different in many details from any previous temples that have existed in Isra'el.

It is surprising that many interpreters failed to take

this temple literally, stating it is just an allegory. If that were really correct, then why would Ezekiel describe this temple in such mind-numbing literal detail? Similar detail is used to denote the specifics of many major items in the Tanakh, such as Noah's Ark, Moses' Tabernacle, and Solomon's Temple. The best conclusion is that if these three accounts are all literal, then there is no reason NOT to assume Ezekiel's temple is literal.

In a vision, Ezekiel described the Temple around 570 B.C.E. None of the previous temples or the plans for the Third Temple matches Ezekiel's vision. Moreover, the Temple and the temple district he describes are not within Jerusalem, but Shiloh, the capital city of Isra'el *before* the first Temple was built by Solomon, which is approximately 19 miles north of Jerusalem. The description in Ezekiel reads as follows:

> When you divide the land by lot for inheritance, you are to set aside an offering for Adonai, a holy portion of the land. Its length is to be 25,000 [cubits, that is, eight miles] and its width 10,000 [three miles]; this entire region is to be holy. Of this there is to be reserved for the holy place an area 875 [feet] square, with eighty-seven-and-a-half feet for open land around it.

> Alongside this region you are to measure a length of eight [miles] and a width of three [miles]; in it is to be the sanctuary, which will

be especially holy. It is a holy portion of the land; it is for the cohanim who serve in the sanctuary, who approach to minister to Adonai; there will be a place for their houses and a place set aside for the sanctuary.

A portion eight by three [miles] will be owned by the L'vi'im who serve in the house; it will also have twenty [gatekeepers'] rooms. You are to give the city possession of an area, alongside the offering of the holy portion, one-and-a-half by eight [miles]; it will be for the whole house of Isra'el. [Note: Ezekiel's cubit was not the normal 18 inch cubit, but a long cubit, 20.679 (or 21) inches.]

The prince is to have the territory on both sides of the holy offering and the city's holding; it will extend westward to the western border of the land and eastward to its eastern border; and the length [from the far side of one] of its two parts [to the far side of the other] will be the same as the length of one of the [tribal] portions.

His possession in Isra'el will be limited to this, and henceforth my princes will not wrong my people but will give the land to the house of Isra'el according to their tribes.

-- Ezekiel 45:1-8 (CJB)

Mashiach

Also, "the perimeter of [the city] will be just under six [miles] long. And from that day on the name of the city will be Adonai Shamah [Adonai is there]" (Ezekiel 48:35 CJB).

The idea of a Fourth Temple certainly is an intriguing one! According to several scholars who are studying the possibility of a 'Fourth' Temple, they say it is designed to be a teaching center that will be used by Mashiach to instruct us about the infinite holiness of G-d and how to properly worship him.

In general, the book of Ezekiel has been overlooked by several scholars. To better understand this new idea, here's a quick look at Ezekiel. Ezekiel had long planned to become a priest in the First Temple when he came of age. But it was not to be. King Nebuchadnezzar raided Jerusalem and after a brief invasion he drove the best out of Jerusalem to Babylon as the following verse describes:

> He carried all Yerushalayim away captive—all the princes, all the bravest soldiers—10,000 captives; also all the craftsmen and metalworkers. No one was left but the poorest people of the land. -- 2 Kings 24:14 (CJB)

During his fifth year of exile from Jerusalem in 593 B.C.E., G-d called Ezekiel to become a prophet to the house of Isra'el which continued until 570 B.C.E. The Temple about which Ezekiel prophesied takes eight chapters to describe in details of what he saw.

Another event Ezekiel foresaw in his vision was the actual departure of Shekinah, the dwelling place of G-d, from the Temple of Solomon, (Ezekiel 9:1-11:25). Then eighteen years later, Ezekiel received a vision of Jerusalem, a future view of the return of the Shekinah to Isra'el and to the Temple (43:1-12). This glorious day of return was also seen by the prophet Isaiah:

> On that day, Adonai's plant will be beautiful and glorious; and the fruit of the land will be the pride and splendor of Isra'el's survivors. Those left in Tziyon and remaining in Yerushalayim will be called holy and everyone in Yerushalayim written down for life.
>
> When Adonai washes away the filth of the women of Tziyon and cleanses Yerushalayim from the bloodshed in it with a blast of searing judgment, Adonai will create over the whole site of Mount Tziyon and over those who assemble there a smoking cloud by day and a shining, flaming fire by night; for the Glory will be over everything like a hupah. A sukkah will give shade by day from the heat; it will also provide refuge and cover from storm and rain.   -- Isaiah 4:2-6 (CJB)

In addition to being a very large and complex structure, the features of Ezekiel's temple differ in several unique ways from any previously existing Jewish temple. These have been catalogued by

Mashiach

researcher John Schmitt, a Portland, Oregon Bible scholar, as follows:

- No wall of partition to exclude Gentiles.
- No Court of Women
- No Laver (see Ezekiel 36:24-27)
- No Table of Shewbread (see Micah 5:4)
- No Lampstand or Menorah (see Isaiah 49:6)
- No Golden Altar of Incense (Zechariah 8:20-23)
- No Veil (Isaiah 25:6-8)
- No Ark of the Covenant (Jeremiah 3:16)
- Sacrificial Altar to be accessed from the East

The following page shows an interpretive drawing of the Temple layout described by Ezekiel courtesy of Lambert Dolphin and Templemount.org:

EZEKIEL'S TEMPLE, COURTS, WALLS, AND GATES

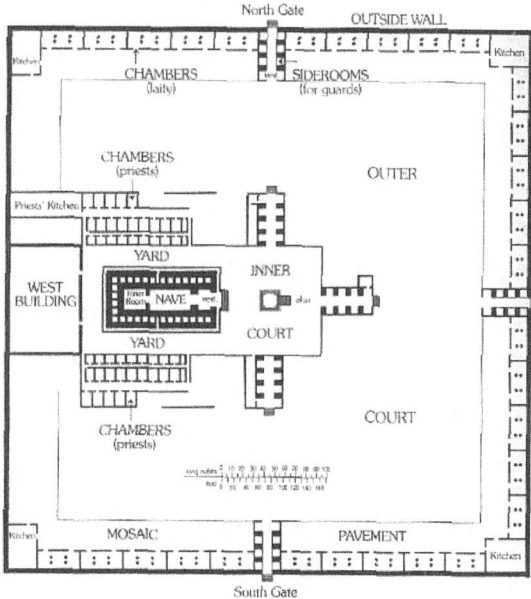

Courtesy Lambert Dolphin & templemount.org

So will Mashiach build a Temple?

It certainly appears that he will, and it will most likely be Ezekiel's description of this Fourth Holy Temple.

Mashiach

Chapter 6
Ingathering of the Jewish Exiles

The third tradition states that when Mashiach is reigning as King of Isra'el, the Jews will be ingathered from their exile and return to Isra'el, their homeland. Moses states in Deuteronomy 30:5 (CJB): "Adonai your G-d will bring you back into the land your ancestors possessed, and you will possess it; he will make you prosper there, and you will become even more numerous than your ancestors."

This "collection of people" appears also in Isaiah 11:11-12 as follows:

On that day Adonai will raise his hand again, a second time, to reclaim the remnant of his people who remain from Ashur, Egypt, Patros, Ethiopia, Eilam, Shin'ar, Hamat and the islands in the sea. He will hoist a banner for the Goyim, assemble the dispersed of Isra'el, and gather the scattered of Y'hudah from the

four corners of the earth.
                    -- Isaiah 11:11-12 (CJB)

Other verses announcing a mass summons from Yahweh appear in Jeremiah 30:3, 32:37; and Ezekiel 11:17; 36:24). To fully understand why there will be an ingathering, we need to explore and understand why we the Jewish people were expelled from Judea in the first place.

While exploring this tradition, I encountered an important question: Have we Jews been blinded to Mashiach? Even before the destruction of the temple in 70 C.E., the people of Isra'el had been turning away from YHWH and becoming a secular society. Some would even describe this "turning away" as the beginning of a pagan society! The great military prowess Isra'el had enjoyed under King David was long gone, until 1948, when the modern day Isra'el was created. Prior to 1948, Isra'el was a dependent state ruled by foreigners for centuries. Still, during the first decades of the C.E., there was a respectable Temple in Jerusalem. Sacrifices and offerings and the formalities of our religion were still there.

However, our priesthood was corrupt. K.H. Tan describes in his book, *The Zion Traditions*, evidence of this corruption provided by Josephus in AJ 14.110. The Temple had amassed to itself great wealth through the diaspora Jews. Josephus describes the fact that the priests' and Zealots' debts were burnt instead of repaid. Tithes were forcibly extracted from the people. Other corruptions also occurred on the part of the Temple

Mashiach

establishment before the Temple's destruction in 70 C.E. The outstanding example is found in b.Pesh.57a, which reads:

Woe unto me because of the house of
Baithos [Boethus];
woe unto me for their lances [or 'evil-speaking']!

Woe unto me because of the house of Hanin,
woe unto me for their whisperings [of 'calumnies']!

Woe unto me because of the house of Qathros
woe unto me because of their reed pens!

Woe unto me because of the house of
Ishmael b. Phiabe,
woe unto me because of their fist!

For they are high priests and their sons are treasurers
and their sons-in-law are temple overseers,
and their servants smite the people with sticks.

Tan goes on to say: "The four families mentioned supplied most of the high priests from the reign of Herod the Great to the fall of Jerusalem." Another of Tans' quotes substantiates Temple corruption. "This data comports well with the evidence from other Josephus writings and Qumran, demonstrating corruption on the part of the Temple establishment..." Tan quotes several other incidents with references

D.A. Osterman

supporting the wide spread corruption in the Temple.

The number was quite small of those who were faithful to the G-d of Abraham and Isaac. Thankfully, a precious few remained faithful to YHWH.

Calculations by Jewish biblical scholars conclude that on August 10, in C.E. 70, the 9th of Av, on the exact anniversary *day* when the King of Babylon burned Solomon's Temple in 586 B.C.E., the Temple burned again. G-d allowed Titus the Roman General, who would later become Caesar, to take the city and burn the Temple to the ground.

Jewish historian, Flavius Josephus gave a detailed account of Titus' soldiers' monstrous conduct. Josephus reported no other city had ever endured such horrors, nor fathered such depravity. As the vast majority of the Jewish population of the day watched the Temple burn and could do nothing to stop it, many sympathetic Romans were moved to tears. Just as Daniel had predicted, the Temple was destroyed. Yet in Daniel 9, the prophet showed us that Mashiach would come before the destruction of Herod's temple as written:

> Know, therefore, and discern that seven weeks [of years] will elapse between the issuing of the decree to restore and rebuild Yerushalayim until **an anointed prince comes**. It will remain built for sixty-two weeks [of years], with open spaces and moats; but these will be troubled times. Then, after the sixty-two weeks, Mashiach will be cut off and have

70

nothing. The people of a prince yet to come will destroy the city and the sanctuary, but his end will come with a flood, and desolations are decreed until the war is over. He will make a strong covenant with leaders for one week [of years]. For half of the week he will put a stop to the sacrifice and the grain offering. On the wing of detestable things the desolator will come and continue until the already decreed destruction is poured out on the desolator.   -- Daniel 9:25-27 (CJB)

The destruction of the Temple and the city of Jerusalem was clearly a demonstration of the anger of our G-d at the Jewish people, the majority of whom had become ungodly and secular or even pagan. Our Jewish ancestors were driven into exile and became wanderers in foreign lands. We were a people without a country. For nineteen centuries we would be dispersed and persecuted.

It was G-d who scattered us, his chosen people. However, He had an ultimate purpose in doing so, even if the purpose was certainly uncomfortable for us to endure. The Jews were to be a blessing to each city in which we were scattered around the globe; and, thereafter, we were meant to be re-gathered by G-d at the right time.

This brings us to today, modern times, and the 21st century. The Ingathering has clearly not been completed; but as mentioned in Chapter 3, a particularly bright spot on the world stage is this portion of the prophet's prediction that has to a great extent already being fulfilled. Six million of our Jewish people have returned to Isra'el thus far, and these early settlers have made the barren land to bloom again. Still many of the returning Jews are simply secular and not believers in the work that G-d is doing for his people.

This re-birth of Isra'el is indeed a promise from our G-d fulfilled. The fact that our people could be dispersed all over the world and survive as a people for 1900 years, and then have David Ben-Gurion on May 14, 1948, proclaim the creation of the modern day Jewish State of Isra'el must certainly be considered a miracle unmatched in modern times.

However, many Jews still believe that because this modern day ingathering of the Jews from the Diaspora came before the reign of Mashiach it doesn't really begin to fulfill this prophecy.

Who WILL accomplish this miracle? According to "Blessing Ten of the Amidah," the Shemoneh Esreh Prayer, "Kibbutz Galuyot" (Ingathering of Exiles), G-d will "sound the great shofar for freedom" and lift up the banner to gather our exiles back from the corners of the globe just BEFORE Mashiach's coming. This is one of the amazing prophecies, from G-d, redeeming His people. G-d's restitution will come quickly. This return of the Isra'elites from exile will be a victorious parade.

The prophecies, however, raise another unanswered question: Will all the Children of Isra'el return? Or only the Jews from the tribe of Judah? Once again, we must look at two differing views. The

Mashiach

Mishnah has determined that the greater part of The Ten Tribes shall not return again, for it is written in the Torah:

> ...and Adonai, in anger, fury and incensed with indignation, uprooted them from their land and threw them out into another land — as it is today. -- Deuteronomy 29:27 (CJB)

Rabbi Akiba, who most agree is the father of rabbinical Judaism, supports the Mishnah's declaration as follows:

> As this day goes and returns not, so do they go and return not. Plainly put, Rabbi Akiba is of the opinion that the Ten Tribes will not re-gather in Isra'el for Mashiach's appearance.

A second school of thought regarding all dispersed Jews returning to the Homeland is stated by Rabbi Eliezer, author of around 300 laws in the Mishnah:

> Like as this day: as the day grows dark and then becomes light, so also with the Ten Tribes; now they are in darkness, but in the future there shall be light for them.

Here we have two of our most revered Rabbinic Scholars holding completely opposite points of view. In addition to the two opinions, the anonymous Baraitha (a tradition in the Jewish oral law not incorporated in the Mishnah) is quoted plainly and without controversy: "The land of Isra'el will in time to come be divided between thirteen tribes." Why thirteen tribes and not twelve?

Jacob (Isra'el) had twelve sons: Reuben, Simeon, Levi, Judah, Dan, Naphtali, Gad, Asher, Issachar, Zebulun, Joseph, and Benjamin (Genesis 29:32 - 30:24 and Genesis 35:18). However the twelves tribes turned into thirteen when Jacob gave Joseph a "double portion."

Despite the respect Rabbi Akiba enjoys historically, Rabbi Eliezer's opinion is generally the one that is accepted today as correct. Furthermore, according to Talmudic teaching and general Tannaitic (the time period from 70 C.E. - 225 C.E.) opinion, all the tribes of Isra'el will return to their native country and enjoy a portion of the land of their ancestors. G-d's purpose in this is to fulfill the promise he made to Abraham and his descendants with regard to inheritance of the land:

> That day Adonai made a covenant with Avram:
>
> I have given this land to your descendants — from the Vadi of Egypt to the great river, the Euphrates River — the territory of the Keni, the K'nizi, the Kadmoni, the Hitti, the P'rizi, the Refa'im, the Emori, the Kena'ani, the Girgashi and the Y'vusi.'
>
> -- Genesis 15:18-21 (CJB)

Mashiach

He describes the territory in Ezekiel's prophesies:

Adonai Elohim says this: 'These are the borders of the land you are to distribute for inheritance by the twelve tribes of Isra'el, with Yosef receiving two portions. For inheritance you will each have equal shares. I swore to your ancestors that I would give them this land, and now it falls to you to inherit it.

The borders of the land will be as follows: on the north, from the Great Sea through Hetlon to the entrance of Tz'dad, Hamat, Berotah, Sibrayim (which is between the border of Dammesek and the border of Hamat), Hatzer-Hatikhon (which is toward the border of Havran). The border from the sea will be Hatzar-'Einon (at the border of Dammesek); while on the north, northward, is the border of Hamat. This is the north side.'
-- Ezekiel 47:13-17 (CJB)

Here is an approximation of what the map would look like in accordance with Ezekiel's prophecy:

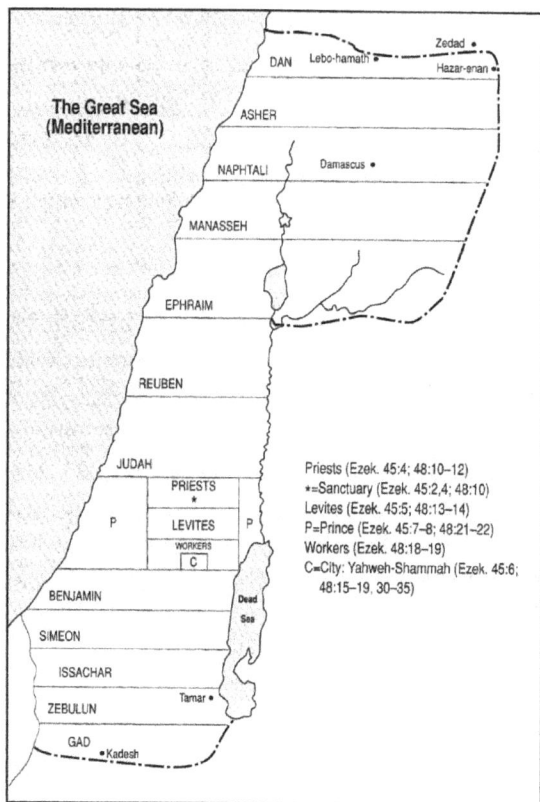

Courtesy Lambert Dolphin & templemount.org

On the east side, measure between Havran and 'Dammesek, Gil'ad and the land of Isra'el by the Yarden, from the border to the eastern sea. This is the east side.

On the side of the Negev toward the south it will be from Tamar as far as the waters of M'rivot-Kadesh, then to the Vadi [of Egypt] and on to the Great Sea. This is the south side toward the Negev.

The west side will be the Great Sea, as far as across from the entrance to Hamat. This is the west side.

This is the territory you are to divide among the tribes of Isra'el.'
-- Ezekiel 47:18-21 (CJB)

An interesting side note is called for here. During the Kingdom of G-d when Mashiach will reign from Isra'el, the Brit Chadasha book of Revelation lists 12 tribes. Even though the map above shows a portion of the land that will go the tribe of Dan, it is conspicuously missing from the list in Revelation. No one seems to know exactly why Dan was omitted. Some assume Dan was removed due to its idolatry (Judges 18:30-31) and then Manasseh was added to fill Dan's place to keep the number twelve. Possibly the return of Levi and exclusion of Dan indicates that the Levitical priesthood was over and original election according to the flesh really did not matter anymore. In any event, this is truly odd and must have some symbolic meaning.

Many scholars today still question why the Jews

must first be gathered before Mashiach returns. One purpose of this ingathering parallels the prophecy earlier in the book of Ezekiel which declares that the Jews must first be gathered in "unbelief" as the following verses describe:

> I will bring you out from the peoples and gather you out of the countries where you were scattered, with a mighty hand, with a stretched-out arm and with poured-out fury; then I will bring you into the desert of the peoples and judge you face to face. Just as I judged your ancestors in the desert of the land of Egypt, so will I judge you, says Adonai Elohim. I will make you pass under the crook and bring you into the obligations of the covenant. I will rid you of the rebels who are in revolt against me—I will bring them out from the land where they are living, but they will not enter the land of Isra'el; then you will know that I am Adonai.
> -- Ezekiel 20:34-38 (CJB)

These passages suggest the purpose of the 1948 creation of the state of Isra'el was to purge out the dissenters by having them pass under a rod of grief. For us Jews with a view towards Isra'el and the current display of hostilities in the Middle East, we should be concerned—indeed afraid.

Ezekiel 22:17-22 further defines this judgment as purging the unbelievers from Isra'el. G-d will use a

Mashiach

period of tribulation to purge out secular Jews through the refining fire of His wrath, and sift out the redeemed remnant of Jews for salvation at the end of the aharit ha-yamim (End Time) tribulation period described in Daniel's "Seventieth Week."

G-d even goes so far as to reveal the number of unbelievers which will be destroyed in Zechariah as described:

> In time, throughout that land, says Adonai, **two-thirds of those in it will be destroyed—** they will die, but one-third will remain. That third part I will bring through the fire; I will refine them as silver is refined, I will test them as gold is tested. They will call on my name, and I will answer them. I will say, This is my people and they will say, Adonai is my G-d.
> -- Zechariah 13:8-9 (CJB)

So when the nation of Isra'el was restored in 1948, we can be assured that G-d is setting the stage for the prophetic events for the return of Mashiach, and that a period of tribulation must be endured prior to his arrival.

So will Mashiach gather the Jews from around the world and rule and reign from Isra'el? It appears that will be the case. Still, it is not without fear and trepidation, and trials by fire that will destroy two-thirds of the people of Isra'el that our future holds in these last days as we await Mashiach.

Chapter 7
Observance of the Torah
Embraced by All Jews

The forth tradition states that Mashiach will reign as King at a time when all the Jewish people will observe G-d's commandments.

This tradition clearly has not occurred at this time and will happen either sometime after Mashiach appears or just before His arrival. What I really found interesting was that for this tradition of Mashiach to be fulfilled depends entirely on us, the Jewish people and our moral regeneration. In other words, Isra'el's salvation depends on Isra'el itself. Clearly the prophet Hosea predicted Mashiach would return when all Jews embrace the Torah and admit their guilt, as the following verses describe:

> I will go and return to my place, till they admit their guilt and search for me, seeking me

Mashiach

eagerly in their distress." Come, let us return to Adonai; for he has torn, and he will heal us; he has struck, and he will bind our wounds. After two days, he will revive us; on the third day, he will raise us up; and we will live in his presence.   -- Hosea 5:15-6:2 (CJB)

The first part of this verse is the operative subject: "I will go and return to my place." In order for that to be true and accurate, a rhetorical question must be answered: "Go from and return to where? Obviously it is here, Isra'el. There needs to be a coming of Mashiach - twice for this prophecy to be true. However, many Jews today claim that the Jewish Bible offers absolutely no evidence to support the Christian doctrine of a Second Coming. Yet the Tanakh seems to be clear that this will happen in the end times, when Mashiach declares:

...and I will pour out on the house of David and on those living in Yerushalayim a spirit of grace and prayer; and they will look to me, whom they pierced." They will mourn for him as one mourns for an only son; they will be in bitterness on his behalf like the bitterness for a firstborn son.   -- Zechariah 12:10 (CJB)

Even though most Jews agree with the opinion that there is no evidence in the Tanakh that shows a Second Coming, if we look to rabbinic tradition, we see our rabbis too have had difficulties with this issue. The

D.A. Osterman

Tanakh prophets portrayed a picture of Mashiach ruling and reigning while freeing Isra'el, thus ending all war and an all-inclusive knowledge of G-d (Isaiah 2:1-4, Isaiah 11:1-9, Ezekiel 40-48, Daniel 2:44, Zechariah 14). At the same time, it is hard to ignore all the other prophecies that speak of Mashiach suffering as an atonement for sin (Psalm 22, Isaiah 52:13-53:12, Daniel 9:25-26, Zechariah 12:10). How does a rabbi arbitrate between these two pictures of Mashiach?

Obviously G-d's plan wouldn't (couldn't) include a Mashiach that failed on his first attempt in which He needed to send Mashiach back to try again. Instead, it shows that YHWH had two different goals, one for each appearance of Mashiach. The first goal was to fulfill the prophecies of the "Suffering Servant." The second goal clearly indicates that while Mashiach didn't bring the anticipated (and certainly desired) lasting peace, this does not invalidate the fact the He is indeed the "Anointed One" and Moshi'a of Isra'el. Simply put, G-d's plan was for Mashiach to come twice, the first time as a blood sacrifice to die for our sins, and the second time returning as the Judge and King to "Rule and Reign" over all of the Earth.

Mashiach will return when all people and all ethnic groups, worldwide, worship the G-d of Abraham, Isaac, and Jacob. Just as in the book of Hosea, we can read more about the appearance of Mashiach and the restoration of the nation of Isra'el. Adonai-Tzva'ot says:

> When that time comes, ten men will take hold
> — speaking all the languages of the nations —

Mashiach

will grab hold of the cloak of a Jew and say,
"We want to go with you, because we have
heard that G-d is with you."
-- Zechariah 8:23 (CJB)

Then Adonai will be king over the whole
world. On that day Adonai will be the only
one, and his name will be the only name.
-- Zechariah 14:9 (CJB)

But does this precept that all people observe G-d's
commandments require that all Jews (and Gentiles)
observe all of the 613 Mitzvot commandments
completely? That seems hardly practical and very
improbable that *every* Jew and *every* Gentile will obey
all 613 Mitzvot commandments perfectly.

Today, most agree that Zechariah was referring to
what are called the "Noahide Laws." These much more
uncomplicated and elegant commands of G-d are a
binding set of moral imperatives, that were given to the
"children of Noah" - that is all of humanity, rather than
trying to squeeze every human into conformity with
today's the 613 commandments.

These seven Noahide Laws are:

1. Do Not Deny G-d
2. Do Not Blaspheme G-d
3. Do Not Murder
4. Do Not Engage in Incestuous, Adulterous or
   Homosexual Relationships

5. Do Not Steal
6. Do Not Eat of a Live Animal
7. Establish Courts/Legal System to Ensure Law Obedience

Maimonides rules that Moses was commanded by Elohim to compel the world to accept these seven commandments. For many centuries, however, the circumstances did not allow this to be done.

Rabbi Menachem M. Schneerson declared in 1983, it was time to revitalize this long-dormant aspect and role of the Jewish people. Four years later in 1987, President Ronald Reagan, a close friend of the Rabbi and longtime supporter, signed a proclamation speaking of "the historical tradition of ethical values and principles, which have been the bedrock of society from the dawn of civilization when they were known as the Seven Noahide Laws, transmitted through G-d to Moses on Mount Sinai." Upon receiving notification of the Joint Resolution of the United States Congress and President Reagan's proclamation, Rabbi Schneerson wrote to the President:

> ... By focusing attention on "the ancient ethical principles and moral values which are the foundation of our character as a nation," and on the time-honored truth that "education must be more than factual enlightenment - it must enrich the character as well as the mind," while reaffirming the eternal validity of these G-d given Seven Noahide Laws (with all their ramifications) for people of all faiths - you

Mashiach

have expressed most forcefully the real spirit
of the American nation ... .

While the world certainly is yet to accept these
seven commandments, steps like these by the United
States are encouraging.

In spite of this some still insist that the 613 Mitzvot
commandments be strictly adhered to. The Law itself is
not bad as it defines sin. It is the misuse of the Law,
and the way that human traditions can end up
supplanting the Law, that are bad. Adding the laws of
men to the pure revelation of G-d is a mistake.

> In order to obey the mitzvot of Adonai your
> G-d which I am giving you, do not add to what
> I am saying, and do not subtract from it.
> -- Deuteronomy 4:2 (CJB)

But the rabbis have added many rules to the Word
of G-d given to Moses. These manmade traditions have
complicated and confused things, and helped us miss
the true goal of the Torah and the Tanakh regarding
Mashiach.

The prophet Jeremiah put it this way:

> For my people have committed two evils: they
> have abandoned me, the fountain of living
> water, and dug themselves cisterns, broken
> cisterns, that can hold no water!
> -- Jeremiah 2:13 (CJB)

85

D.A. Osterman

By adding manmade rules to the Torah and Tanakh, by elevating rabbinic writings to the same level as G-d's Word, and by taking away from the Word of G-d by not accepting Mashiach; the rabbis have done terrible spiritual damage to the Jewish people.

While it is certainly true, most of the civilized world now agrees that the principles of the Law, especially the Ten Commandments, are the bedrock of civilization. Yet the fact remains that for the last two thousand years it has been impossible for the Jewish people to observe **all** the commandments of the Law of Moses as many are intent upon needing a Temple, the priesthood, animal sacrifices, and living together as a homogeneous theocratic country within the borders of Isra'el.

The Reform Judaism movement of the last 250 years represents the largest percentage of Jewish congregations today. Many times this movement regards "the Law" as being out of date; stating "the Law" still contains interesting historic qualities. Even the Conservative Judaism movement agrees that it's impossible to observe **all** the commandments and attain complete holiness and oneness with G-d and perfection.

With these facts in mind and the apparent impossibility of there being a strict adherence to ALL of the Laws in the Torah, we must look for a different answer to our early traditions. Many, and I support them, have suggested the efforts put forward by Rabbi Menachem M. Schneerson in 1983 with the support of President Reagan regarding Noahide Laws, we have already begun to accomplish this requirement for the appearance of Mashiach.

Mashiach

Chapter 8
Universal Knowledge of G-d

The fifth tradition states that Mashiach will rule at a time when all the people of the world will come to acknowledge and serve the one true G-d (Zechariah 3:9, 8:23,14:9,16; Isaiah 45:23; Jeremiah 31:33; Ezekiel 38:23; Psalm 86:9). Mashiach shall mend the entire world population so that everyone shall serve G-d in unity. While there are many passages in the Tanakh which describe this, the main Tanakh passage Judaism scholars used to create this requirement is found in the book of Jeremiah as follows:

> Here, the days are coming," says Adonai, when I will make a new covenant with the house of Isra'el and with the house of Y'hudah. It will not be like the covenant I made with their fathers on the day I took them by their hand and brought them out of the land of Egypt; because they, for their part, violated

my covenant, even though I, for my part, was a husband to them, says Adonai. "For this is the covenant I will make with the house of Isra'el after those days," says Adonai: "I will put my Torah within them and write it on their hearts; I will be their G-d, and they will be my people. **No longer will any of them teach his fellow community member or his brother, 'Know Adonai;' for all will know me, from the least of them to the greatest; because I will forgive their wickednesses and remember their sins no more.**

-- Jeremiah 31:30-34 (CJB)

Thus, "everyone" will "know" Him, will see Him, hear His voice, and watch His realm manifest here on Earth.

It is clear that we have not yet seen this period of human history unfold. There are billions of people in the world today who are atheistic or adhere to paganistic or some kind of polytheistic religion. Not all the people of the world will come to acknowledge and serve the one true G-d until after the arrival of Mashiach.

The main difficulty most Jews have today understanding this prophecy is the concept of two appearances of Mashiach. While it is true that the exact phrase "second coming" is not found in either the Jewish or even the Christian Bible, it is disingenuous to claim that no concept of the second coming exists in Scripture. If we believe there is only one "capital-M" Mashiach, then it is reasonable to think He would come twice because there are two distinct pictures of Him

Mashiach

given in Scripture. There is the "Suffering Servant" appearance, followed by the "Reign and Rule" kingdom which is a much more accurate understanding of the prophecy in the Tanakh.

In Judaism, the servant Messiah is called Mashiach ben Yosef (Mashiach son of Joseph), in reference to the servant pictured by Joseph at the end of the book of Genesis. The book of Daniel refers to Mashiach being "cut off" just as Joseph was cut off from his family. There are numerous parallels between Joseph and Mashiach.

The sovereign Mashiach is called Mashiach ben David (Mashiach son of David) in reference to the reigning sovereign pictured by King David. Numerous passages refer to the authority and kingdom of David, yet David did not receive the fullness of those promises. Those promises find their fulfillment in the coming Mashiach and Judaism recognizes this as well.

Isra'el has had an extra privilege and responsibility. Picked by G-d as His covenant nation, our destiny was above all others to make G-d's plan and message known to the whole world. To quote the promise G-d made to Abraham in Genesis 12:2 (CJB): "I will make of you a great nation, I will bless you, and I will make your name great; and you are to be a blessing." **We,** the Jewish people, are to be the light of the world.

Distressing as it was for us to live through, G-d scattered us—his chosen people—because He had an ultimate purpose. We Jews were to be a blessing to each city in which we were scattered around the globe.

D.A. Osterman

We are to spread an understanding of YHWH, and then finally be re-gathered by G-d at the right time. G-d's time.

Here is an interesting story that applies to our assignment by G-d to become the "light of the world" in a book written by author George Sweeting, in his book *The No-Guilt Guide for Witnessing*, tells of a man by the name of David Mendelsohn who in 1949 was found guilty of murder and sentenced to life in prison.. It was a true story, telling of an American criminal [I have changed the names and places]:

> An American man by the name of David Mendelsohn who in 1942 was found guilty of murder and sentenced to life in prison. Later for exceptionally good behavior he was transferred and paroled to work on a farm in Minnesota in a remote northeastern part of the state.
>
> In 1962 almost 20 years after his initial incarceration, Mendelsohn's sentence was terminated, and a letter bearing the good news was sent to him. But David never saw the letter, nor was he told anything about it. Minnesota was known for its severe winters with numerous days of sub-zero temperatures. Life was very hard. He certainly had no chance of a future in this remote part of the country. But David kept doing what he had been instructed to do, year after year, even when the farmer for whom he worked, died.

Mashiach

Another Ten years went by when finally a state parole officer learned about Mendelsohn's plight, found him, and told him that his sentence had been terminated. He was a free man.

The moral of the story is found in one simple question. Would it matter to you if someone sent you an important message—the most important announcement in your life—and year after year the urgent message was never delivered?

We Jews know the truths G-d has sent to us through His many prophets. We are to be a blessing to each city in which we were scattered around the globe and to each person we meet along our journeys through life. But the question remains: Are we doing all we can to make sure that people around us get the message?

Sadly for most of us, while the truth has come true in the form of the writing and preserving the Word of G-d by Jewish men who are proclaiming G-d's Word, not all of us are being a blessing to people we meet daily. We have not been preparing the world for the arrival of the Mashiach. When Mashiach does arrive, we will confess the words in Isaiah 26:18: "We have not brought salvation to the Earth; we have not given birth to people of the world." That is, Isra'el has not made G-d's blessings known as He wanted those blessings known. We will be required to answer for our actions, or inactions. "If you will not do this, then you have sinned against Adonai, and you must understand that your sin will find you out" (Numbers 32:23 CJB).

And why is it that we don't tell those around us about the truths of G-d we have been so fortunate to learn and understand? There are ten typical excuses we use:

1. 90% failed in the past when we tried to tell others about G-d
2. We do not know what the Tanakh says, so we don't know what we should say or do
3. We feel we should just leave it to the Rabbi and other professionals
4. We don't want to impose our Jewish faith on others
5. They may ask a question I can't answer
6. Simple, I'm scared
7. "I don't speak well"
8. We don't know how to start a conversation about G-d
9. People may remember the bad things I have done
10. I don't have time

Are these really the excuses we plan to give to Mashiach when we are required to answer for ourselves?

As the only true King and Judge, G-d has a *Sefer HaChayim* (Book of Life) as well as a *Sefer Ha-Metim* (Book of Death). David gives one example, "Your eyes could see me as an embryo, but in your **book** all my days were already written; my days had been shaped before any of them existed" (Psalm 139:16).

Mashiach

The scriptures clearly warn that after the arrival of Mashiach on the Day of Judgment to come, anyone's name not found in His Book of Life will be condemned and destroyed. "When that time comes, Mikha'el, the great prince who champions your people, will stand up; and there will be a time of distress unparalleled between the time they became a nation and that moment. At that time, your people will be delivered, everyone whose name is found written in the **book** (Daniel 12:1). There is a Divine Book, and the name of every human is in it.

So while this tradition and requirement of a genuine Mashiach for global and "Universal Knowledge of G-d," is correct, it is certainly obvious that this won't happen until after Mashiach has defeated the enemies of Isra'el and brought judgment to those who deserve it.

Chapter 9
Mashiach from the Tribe of Judah
Descendant of King David AND
King Solomon

The sixth and final criterion in Jewish tradition states in the Tanakh that Mashiach must be a member of the tribe of Judah (Genesis 49:10) and a direct descendant of both King David and King Solomon (2 Samuel 7:12-14; 1 Chronicles 22:9-10). Genealogy in the Bible is only passed down from father to son (Numbers 1:1-18).

The Davidic line, known in Hebrew as Malkhut Beit David, "Royal House of David," refers to the tracing of lineage to the King David as described in the Tanakh. Various verses throughout the Tanakh clearly state that Mashiach will be a descendant of the house of David. The best description of this is contained in the Book of Samuel as follows:

> Moreover, Adonai tells you that Adonai will make you a house. 'When your days come to

94

an end and you sleep with your ancestors, I will establish one of your descendants to succeed you, one of your own flesh and blood; and I will set up his rulership. He will build a house for my name, and I will establish his royal throne forever. I will be a father for him, and he will be a son for me. If he does something wrong, I will punish him with a rod and blows, just as everyone gets punished; nevertheless, my grace will not leave him, as I took it away from Sha'ul, whom I removed from before you. Thus your house and your kingdom will be made secure forever before you; your throne will be set up forever.' Natan told David all of these words and described this entire vision.

-- 2 Samuel 7:11-17 (CJB)

David's acquisition of the throne was conditional as shown above, applying only to his righteous descendants. G-d assures David in Psalms 89:31-38 that his dynasty will last forever as G-d decries in the following verses:

If his descendants abandon my Torah and fail to live by my rulings, if they profane my regulations and don't obey my mitzvot, I will punish their disobedience with the rod and their guilt with lashes. But I won't withdraw my grace from him or be false to my faithfulness. I will not profane my covenant

or change what my lips have spoken. I have sworn by my holiness once and for all; I will not lie to David—his dynasty will last forever, his throne like the sun before me. It will be established forever, like the moon, which remains a faithful witness in the sky. (Selah)
-- Psalm 89:31-38 (CJB)

While this promise seems to be made about all of David's offspring, we find that G-d singles out Solomon in First Chronicles:

But you will have a son who will be a man of rest. I will give him rest from all his enemies that surround him; for his name is to be Shlomo [King Solomon], and during his reign I will give peace and quiet to Isra'el. It is he who will build a house for my name. He will be my son and I will be his father, and I will establish the throne of his kingdom over Isra'el forever. -- 1 Chronicles 22:9-10 (CJB)

Then again, in 1 Chronicles 28:5-6, David repeats:

…And of all my sons—for Adonai has given me many sons—he has chosen Shlomo my son to sit on the throne of the kingdom of Adonai over Isra'el. Moreover, he said to me, 'Shlomo your son will build my house and courtyards, for I have chosen him to be a son to me, and I will be a father to him.'
-- 1 Chronicles 28:5-6 (CJB)

Mashiach

After King David reaffirms that Solomon will reign after him, the Tanakh shows that the Jewish monarchy continues through Solomon: "Let my Lord King David live forever" (1 Kings 1:31, CJB). The above quotes depict and illuminate the Mashiach as a descendant of both David and Solomon. They show a logical progression behind the twelfth of the Jewish fundamental beliefs declared by Maimonides.

The Tanakh should be read as straight forward an explanation as possible and should be accepted as the best interpretation. Yet there are other voices that certainly have credibility and raise good questions to this statement of traditions aside from the Tanakh. In fact, this is where discussion of the genealogy of Mashiach will become somewhat controversial, but worthy of straight-forward discussion and consideration of some of our first century C.E. ancestors' beliefs.

The first century Essene movement of our Jewish faith raised a good question associated with this tradition. They believed in Mashiach Yeshua. However, some of the rabbinical scholars both of their day and today criticized their logic and beliefs, eliminating the possibility that Yeshua is the "Suffering Servant" and the "Reign and Rule" sovereign of a new, Jerusalem-centered global kingdom, the latter obviously not yet brought to fruition because we Jews have not all gathered back together. Yet, as we test the Essenes' theory so as to prove or eliminate their belief that Yeshua was Mashiach, we need to follow their train of evidence and either accept their belief, eliminate it, or hold onto the premise of Yeshua as Mashiach we continue assembling and examining evidence.

The Essenes declared that Yeshua "was a descendent of David." If we are to consider Yeshua as Mashiach, Yeshua's Jewish ancestry is very important in order to establish His legitimacy as the true Mashiach. The prophet Jeremiah was specific when he wrote of the coming of the royal son of David as follows:

> The days are coming," says Adonai, "when I will raise a righteous Branch for David. He will reign as king and succeed; he will do what is just and right in the land. In his days Y'hudah will be saved, Isra'el will live in safety, and the name given to him will be Adonai Tzidkenu [Adonai our righteousness].
> -- Jeremiah 23:5-6 (CJB)

An early first century genealogy of Yeshua was used by the Jewish Essene movement, directly derived from the original, ancient official Temple genealogy records that no longer exist. The Romans burned them along with the Temple in 70 C.E. After considerable study of the official Temple records, the Essene scholars' and rabbis' judgements, concluded in the Dead Sea Scrolls that the official Temple genealogy records proved that Yeshua had descended from David as prophesied. Not only was he qualified, Yeshua was the *only* one who could be qualified as Isra'el's Mashiach. G-d had promised David in 1 Samuel 7:16: "Thus your house and your kingdom will be made secure forever before you; your throne will be set up

Mashiach

forever."

In what became known as "The Crucified Messiah Scroll" was finally released to the public in 1991. The world was astonished to hear that one of the unpublished scrolls included incredible references to a "Messiah" who suffered crucifixion for the sins of men. The scroll was translated by Dr. Robert Eisenman, Professor of Middle East Religions of California State University. He declared, "The text is of the most far-reaching significance."

The scroll identified the Messiah as the "Shoot of Jesse" (King David's father) the "Branch of David," and declared that he was "pierced" and "wounded." The word "pierced" remind us of the Messianic prophecy in Psalms 22:16: "They pierced my hands and feet." The prophet Jeremiah (23:5) said, "I will raise unto David a righteous branch."

This reference pointing clearly to the historical Yeshua of Nazareth began creating shock waves for liberal scholarship that previously assumed that the Brit Chadasha account about Yeshua was a myth. Yeshua is the only one who ever claimed to be Mashiach who was crucified. The genealogies recorded in the Brit Chadasha books of Matthew and Luke; reveal that Yeshua was the only one who could prove by the genealogical records kept in the Temple that He was the lineage of King David as the "Son of Jesse." Since the tragic destruction of the Temple and all of it's records in 70 C.E. it would be impossible for anyone else to ever prove their claim to be the Messiah based on their genealogical descent from King David.

D.A. Osterman

In addition, the same Dead Sea Scroll writer uses both the official Temple genealogy records along with at least forty quotations from the Tanakh and a minimum of sixteen times in his formula to trace Yeshua's qualifying genealogy. Only one line is traced from the beginning to the end of the biblical history, the line of King David. Our Scriptures reveal every name before David (Adam to David) and every name after David (David to Zerubbabel). Since Mashiach was to be of the house of David, this can also be labeled as the messianic line. In fact, these extended genealogies show the human origin of Mashiach. As the Seed of the woman, Mashiach had to come out of humanity. As the Seed of Abraham, Mashiach had to come from the nation of Isra'el. As the Seed of Judah, he had to be of the tribe of Judah. As the Seed of David, he had to be of the family of David.

Tracing this Biblical genealogy trail shows it moving from our father Avraham, down fourteen generations to David, down another fourteen generations to the Babylonian exile, and down again another fourteen generations to "Jacob," the father of Joseph, the husband of Mary by whom Yeshua is born.

There is an interesting difficulty when looking at two different written genealogies of the day. They are the lines of two brothers and the children who are cousins. One said Joseph was the son of Jacob who descended through David's son and successor King Solomon. However, when one examines the other lineage, the writing names Joseph as the son of Heli who descended from David through Nathan, who was also David's son and a brother of Solomon.

Mashiach

While it is clear from all of the Tanakh sources that Mashiach will be a descendant of King Solomon, the Zohar foundational work in the literature of Jewish studies includes commentary on the mystical and scriptural interpretation aspects of our Torah. It is this scriptural critique of the rabbinic literature that forms the elaboration of the Torah we all know as the Midrash.

It is interesting that the Zohar, out of the ten sons of David, focuses on Nathan. Chabad.org notes the brilliant commentary of R' Reuven Margolies on this passage in the Zohar. Zohar states that Mashiach will actually be a descendant of Nathan, a different son of David. Zohar discusses the verse (Isaiah 40:9):

Upon a lofty mountain ascend, you who brings good tidings to Zion.

The Zohar states as follows:

You who bring good tidings to Zion is Hephzibah, the wife of Nathan son of David, who is the mother of Mashiach, Menachem son of Amiel. She shall go out and bring the tidings.

The prominent Jewish scholar and kabbalist of the 20th-century, Rabbi Reuven Margolies, makes his point clear that the Zohar is careful to describe Mashiach as a descendant of Nathan's wife, *not* of Nathan himself. Nathan died childless; and Solomon married Nathan's widow according to the laws of yibum, levirate marriage.

The yibum laws of levirate marriage state that the first son born of the brother and of the widow of the deceased [Nathan] is considered to be a continuation of the dead husband's line. Even though Nathan is a descendant of King Solomon, Mashiach is referred to here as "offspring" of Nathan.

So, if the throne of "his kingdom" is Solomon's, how can we know the identity of the true Mashiach? According to genealogy records, Miriam descends from Nathan, the son of David, *not* Solomon. Adding to this Zohar makes a very interesting statement as follows:

> You that bring good tidings to Zion is Hephzibah, the wife of Nathan son of David, who is the mother of Mashiach, Menachem son of Amiel, who was her descendant. She shall go out and bring the tidings about redemption and she is part of the general meaning of: You that bring good tidings to Zion.
> -- Zohar III:173b, Parashat Shlach Lekha 45:298

Therefore, because Yeshua descended from Miriam (Mary), who also was a descendent of King David through the lineage of Nathan, Yeshua had a legal claim to the throne. The two lines of David both focused on Mashiach.

Before turning to further discussion of the Essenes, there is another interesting fact to examine. Author and researcher, Jacob Neusner is considered controversial

Mashiach

by some, but by others he is considered an extraordinary Jewish scholar. Writing about the first century B.C.E. up until approximately the sixth century C.E., he made an interesting observation. He argued that the earliest versions of Genesis, Exodus, and Numbers which are still used in the contemporary Jewish Bible are the invention of Akiba and the other Rabbis of the day in the second century C.E.

This creates a very compelling misinterpretation of the Tanakh. Akiba and the Rabbis wanted to satisfy the critical desires of the Jews, particularly the Pharisees, just as today many people are more interested in seeking approval from their fellow man than from G-d. At that time in history, the Romans had overtaken all of Jerusalem and destroyed the second Temple in 70 C.E. And eleven years before the destruction of the Temple, King Nebuchadnezzar had taken some 10,000 of the elite among the Jews, including all of the Pharisees, and transplanted them to Babylon in an attempt to weaken Judea and prevent it from rebelling.

The incredible influence of the Pharisees among the masses cannot be understated. They were the most honored in Judaism during that time in history and were by far the most numerous and influential of the Judaism movements. As strict legalists, those particular Pharisees stood for the rigid observance of the letter and forms of the Law, and also for the Traditions. There were some good men among them, no doubt; but for the most part, they were known for their covetousness, self-righteousness and hypocrisy while yielding enormous power in the community.

D.A. Osterman

When the Temple was destroyed by the Romans, multitudes of battered Jewish survivors were forcibly exiled to Babylon. However, they did not come to a completely non-Jewish country. The new exiles arrived at a community that already had synagogues, Jewish hierarchy, Torah academies and other institutions teeming with prophets (including Ezekiel, Daniel and Ezra), scholars and leaders.

With that observation in mind, let us return to the Jewish Essene Movement. The Essenes were first-person witnesses to Yeshua, so their point of view on Mashiach cannot be dismissed out of hand. Like the Messianic Jews and Christians today, the Essenes taught that Yeshua was G-d in human form.

Most Jews of that first century C.E. believed the Essenes were totally mistaken about G-d. Indeed most of our first century Jewish ancestors, except for the Essenes, contended that if Yeshua was the long awaited Mashiach, it would make G-d too small. And if G-d were to assume human form, it would diminish both His unity and His divinity. But the Essenes thought that idea was completely turned upside-down. If one believes G-d cannot assume human form, then that false assumption limits the power of G-d to do what He thinks is needed in order to provide for his chosen people.

The Essenes went on to ask a few simple questions relating to their recognition of Yeshua as Mashiach. If Yeshua is the supernaturally conceived Ben Elohim (Son of G-d) rather than the natural son of Joseph, how could he be 'disqualified' as the Pharisees and Jewish scholars of the day (right up to the present) believe?

Mashiach

Emphasizing the second part of the question: So if G-d himself comes to earth, He is unqualified to be our savior? Making that argument, do today's Jewish scholars know how nonsensical and illogical they sound?

The Essene movement differed from all the other Jewish sects of the day in that they were based totally on the Torah and Tanakh and *not* traditions. They believed that the Torah and Tanakh are supernatural books, divinely inspired by the Creator of the universe.

The Essenes' point was that the Pharisee's rigid thinking of the day, using only traditions as a guide to determine who Mashiach could be was pure nonsense. And if Yeshua was truly the son of G-d then he *can't* be Mashiach was pure nonsense. Using those two illogical conclusions limits our Divine G-d, making G-d unable to bring about Mashiach without the aid of us simple humans. Here's an example. G-d freed our *entire* people, 600,000 of our ancestors (Exodus 14) from Pharaoh's grip with the aid of eighty-year-old Moses, and a staff, or "rod." Moses and his staff also parted a giant body of water and produced water out of a rock. Now, do those miracles sound like a limited G-d incapable of using humans for His purpose?

The Pharisees attempted to limit the power of G-d in order to enhance their own self-proclaimed authority and to maintain their position of power in the eyes of their fellow Jews. Their attempts have extended and obviously succeeded over the centuries. One has to question how any person in today's modern world, with all the knowledge of the past at our fingertips, can accept the Pharisees' legalistic clench to manmade traditions that trump G-d's will and power. We simply cannot, anymore. Furthermore, there is more evidence supporting Mashiach's lineage and identity.

The Jewish Essene Movement's position has become stronger in recent years. While the Dead Sea Scrolls were discovered in 1947, it took several decades for them to be pieced together and translated. And even longer for other scholars to be allowed to study the scrolls, never mind the general public to be made aware of the significance of their discovery. These scrolls brought to light a great deal of information about the precepts and practices of the first century Jews and Essenes. From the date of their discovery and for the next 30 years, the "official team" of a small number of scholars published less than half of the total volume. Starting in 1977, pressure began to build to release the scrolls for public study. But the "official team" continued to refuse the release of the scrolls in what prominent scholar Geza Vermes called "the scandal of the century" for almost another 15 years.

Finally, in 1991, 44 years after their discovery, a major push ensued by biblical scholars backed by an enormous public relations onslaught and threatened lawsuits against the "official team" in Isra'el demanding the release of every unpublished Dead Sea Scroll. As a result of the push, diverse learned scholars around the world were at last allowed to review and study the invaluable 1947 find.

Beginning that year in 1991, Zion Wacholder, a distinguished professor and scholar at Hebrew Union College, performed the surprisingly difficult task of

Mashiach

creating an index-concordance using only an outdated desk top-computer. The world was astonished to hear about one of the unpublished Essene scrolls that has several major references to the "Suffering Servant" Mashiach who had suffered crucifixion for the sins of all men. The scroll has far-reaching significance because it shows the same general framework for Mashiach as the early Judeo-Christians believed. The scroll contained references to "the Prophet Isaiah" and his Mashiach prophecy in Chapter 53 of his book in the Tanakh. This scroll provides an amazing parallel to the Brit Chadasha, detailing the fact that Mashiach would first suffer death and then return to rule Isra'el and the nations at a later time. The interesting discovery of this scroll is the revelation that the Essene writers of this scroll understood the dual role of Mashiach as both "Suffering Servant," and Mashiach who would "Reign and Rule."

Despite these revelations, the original scroll team who had maintained jurisdiction over the scrolls since their discovery in 1947 maintained their 'closed mind' to that obvious discovery and continued to claim that there was no evidence about the early Judeo-Christian movement in the unpublished scrolls. The uncomfortable fact for them and Jewish scholars in general is that the new scroll totally contradicts the "Official Team's" statements. In truth, many knowledgeable scholars of Jewish studies currently believe that this single scroll is completely earth-shaking in its importance. Dr. Norman Golb, Professor of Jewish History at the University of Chicago said: "It shows that contrary to what some of the editors said, there are lots of surprises in the scrolls, and this is one of them."

Whenever there is such flagrant abuse and secrecy as was the case of the first "official team," one must suspect the worst. Someday, we may grasp the fullness of the almost half-century cover-up. Until then we must acknowledge that the unveiling of this complete scroll certainly adds a new highlight to one previous difference between Christian and Jewish conceptions of the promised Mashiach. While Jews believe Mashiach will be a man, similar to Moses, with a sacred mission, Messianic Judaism believes that the Bible teaches that Mashiach would be Ben Elohim or "the Son of G-d."

However, Jewish traditions hold that the concept of a "Son of G-d" violates the primary truth of monotheism found in Deuteronomy 6:4: "Sh'ma, Yisra'el! Adonai Eloheinu, Adonai echad [Hear, Isra'el! Adonai our G-d, Adonai is one]." It is understandable how some adherents to the Jewish traditions would come to this belief as some would point out that the use of the name Elohim starting in Genesis 1:1 in Hebrew is mainly used with the singular verb forms and with adjectives and pronouns in the singular.

However, this contradicts what many other serious Jewish scholars point out that the name Elohim contains a masculine plural ending, but certainly does not mean "gods" when referring to the true G-d of Isra'el. Repeating the Shema, Deuteronomy 6:4, the Creator of all things has revealed Himself to His creation through His personal name YHWH, His general title Elohim, as

Mashiach

well as other names and titles signifying His character. He has revealed that in His divine nature He is an inseparable union (echdut); YHWH is One and there is only one YHWH. "Hear, O Isra'el: YHWH [the L-rd] is our Elohim. He is One YHWH. He alone is YHWH."

This One G-d has manifested Himself to mankind in three divine Persons: HaAv [the Father], HaBen [the Son] and Ruach HaKodesh [the Holy Spirit, literally "Breath"], yet all three manifestations have only one name: the Hashalush HaKadosh, and these three constitute ONE (echad) G-d. Considering this, the Tanakh describes the plurality of the G-dhead.

This concept of the Trinity is essentially the same as the Kabbalistic concept of the ten sefirot, the ten different ways G-d manifests Himself in the world to allow humankind to better understand Jehovah.

A triad G-dhead was fully recognized by our Jewish ancestors in the Essene movement, just as Messianic-Jewish and Christian theologians do today, who claim that Yeshua was the "Son of G-d," and that this claim does not violate Deuteronomy 6:4. Rather, the Essenes believed in the Hashalush HaKadosh, or the 'Trinity,' which shows G-d revealing Himself in three personalities: G-d [YHWH] the Father; Ben Elohim [the Son - known to the Essenes as Yeshua]; and, the Spirit of YHWH [Ruach HaKodesh]. The Trinity just allows us humans to understand and more easily communicate with YHWH, and for a very simple reason; no person can possibly come close to understanding the fullness and greatness of YHWH.

D.A. Osterman

As Judeo-Christians today, the Jewish Essenes considered themselves to be monotheists, and they stated their beliefs in complete conformity to the truth of monotheism of the Torah. There is only one G-d.

And this brings us to the question: Is Mashiach to come born of the Tribe of Judah and a Descendant of King David and King Solomon?

There is a very large school of study in scholarly literature that discusses this tradition. Some have the opinion that Mashiach must be a direct blood descendant of the Tribe of Judah and a descendant of King David, while others point to many reasons why the Yeshua of the Jewish Essene movement could easily qualify in meeting the rigid requirement while at the same time be something other than a direct-line blood descendant of King David. However, in today's Jewish community, the position is always claimed, "If Yeshua is the supernaturally conceived Son of G-d, rather than the natural son of Joseph, he is disqualified by the traditions to be the "real Mashiach." Which in response begs the question: "how could he be 'disqualified'?"

Essentially what today's Jewish community is stating is: "If G-d himself comes to earth, He is unqualified to be our savior." I must say it is very difficult for a logical reasoning person to agree with today's Jewish Biblical exegesis scholars. Logically, it is much more probable that our ancient brethren were correct. Indeed it is difficult to comprehend how today's scholars drew their conclusions without realizing just how nonsensical and illogical they sound, particularly in light of many of the recent revelations

Mashiach

disclosed in the Dead Sea Scrolls.

One of my favorite times in our Shabbat worship services is when we recite or sing the song;, "Ani Maamin," after morning prayers in the synagogue as follows:

ANI MA'AMIN

I believe with complete faith
In the coming of the Messiah, I believe
Believe in the coming of the Messiah
In the coming of the Messiah, I believe
Believe in the coming of the Messiah
And even though he may tarry
Nonetheless I will wait for him
And even though he may tarry
Nonetheless I will wait for him
Nonetheless, I will wait for him
I will wait every day for him to come
Nonetheless, I will wait for him
I will wait every day for him to come
I believe (Ani Ma'amin).

For me personally, I am ready, today, to answer the question at the seat of judgment that every Jew will be required to answer: *"Did you crave the coming of the Mashiach?"*

My answer is a resounding, "Yes!"

We are privileged as Jews to be chosen by G-d and to have the honor of worshiping him daily.

Chapter 10
Fulfilled Prophecies and Two Mashiach

Of the six traditional premises for Mashiach, it seems only two have, or soon will be fulfilled: Ingathering of the Jewish Exiles and the rebuilding of the Holy Temple.

The final ingathering was begun over 100 years ago, but officially began on May 14, 1948 when David Ben-Gurion proclaimed the Jewish State of Isra'el. As of Rosh Hashanah 2014, 6.2 million Jews (now representing 75% of the population) have returned to Isra'el with the total population of the country reaching 8.3 million including 21% Arabs, and 4% non-Arab Christians, Baha'i. When Isra'el was established, there were only a total of 806,000 residents. But with the establishment of the Jewish state, the total population swelled to its first and then second millions in 1949 and 1958 respectively. Out of the 14.2 million Jewish people in the world today, 43% reside in Isra'el.

Mashiach

Many Isra'elis are convinced that the rebuilding of the Temple will commence very soon, and people are working to make that happen. I repeat here a few of the signs of the preparations currently underway.

The Ateret Cohanim, Glory of the Priests, in the Old City has begun to train priests and Levites in the rituals of animal sacrifice as they prepare for the re-establishment of fully functioning temple services.

The Temple Institute, an ultra-orthodox organization mentioned in Chapter 4, has already spent in the neighborhood of one-hundred-five million shekels (27 million dollars) preparing and acquiring the necessary materials for rebuilding the Temple.

In ancient times, to build a structure as magnificent as Solomon's Temple would take many years using older construction techniques. However, with today's modern equipment and techniques, most construction experts agree that the Temple could be built in a year or less, after an agreement has been reached within Judaism experts on the exact location.

All Jews know that it will be constructed on Temple Mount. The Temple's location could be north of the "Dome of the Rock," south of the "Dome," or exactly where the current Muslim mosque resides. All of these locations are controversial politically, particularly if the experts determine that the Temple must be constructed where the current Muslim shrine sits. As these discussions continue, more and more members of the Knesset and numerous rabbis are ascending to the Temple Mount more frequently. In an article appearing in *Haaretz* digital, dated July 12,

2013, authors report a surprising 2013 poll commissioned by the Joint Forum of Temple Mount Organizations. They asked Isra'eli Jews "Are you for or against erecting a Temple on the Temple Mount?" Thirty percent answered in the affirmative, while 45 percent were against the location, and 25 percent said they were not sure. Wherever the location, I join with those who believe that the Holy Temple will be rebuilt during our lifetime.

Today the majority of Jew's are still of the opinion that if an individual fails to fulfill even one of these conditions, then he cannot be the Messiah. Because no one has ever fulfilled the Tanakh's description of this future King, most Jews still await the coming of Mashiach. All past Messianic claimants, including Yeshua of Nazareth, Bar Cochba and Shabbtai Tzvi have been rejected.

But is that a correct statement? What about the belief that Mashiach shall come twice?

The issue of "two comings" of Mashiach is not an unusual Jewish thought. For two millennia the rabbinical community has been considering, wondering, and pondering how to solve the differences between the two Mashiach in the various prophecies in the Tanakh. This prophecy states that Mashiach will be rejected despised and killed and then come again to bring Isra'el its long awaited reigning king.

Our Jewish apologists who deny the coming of Mashiach twice are cherry-picking the messianic prophecies. They keep trying to make a defendable claim that there could not be two comings of Mashiach. I paraphrase their defense: "Our Mashiach doesn't

Mashiach

need to come twice to complete the job."

Chapter 2 above discusses "The Anointed One." Scripture provides a straight-forward picture of a "returning King:" "I will go and return to my place, till they admit their guilt and search for me, seeking me eagerly in their distress" (Hosea 5:15, CJB).

In reviewing the Tanakh again regarding at least four of the requirements which are the subject of this book, Mashiach must do the following:

- Build the Third [or Fourth] Temple (Ezekiel 37:26-28).
- Gather all Jews back to the Land of Isra'el (Isaiah 43:3-6).
- Usher in an era of world peace, and end all hatred, oppression, suffering, and disease. As it says: "Nation shall not lift up sword against nation, neither shall man learn war anymore" (Isaiah 2:4).
- Spread universal knowledge of the G-d of Isra'el, which will unite humanity as one. As it says: "G-d will be King over all the world—on that day, G-d will be One and His Name will be One" (Zechariah 14:9).

As mentioned previously, the Hebrew word Mashiach (מׁשׁיׁח) is extremely rare in the writings of the Prophets. This word is only found once in Isaiah, once in Lamentations, twice in Daniel, and once in Habakkuk. None of the verses in the bullet points above state that Mashiach would do any of these things.

D.A. Osterman

If one looks closely again, all these prophecies only say that Adonai our G-d will accomplish them, not Mashiach as follows:

- I am **Adonai**, who sets Isra'el apart as holy, when my sanctuary is with them forever;

- For I am **Adonai**, your G-d… I will say to the north, 'Give them up!' and to the south, 'Don't hold them back!' Bring my sons from far away, and my daughters from the ends of the earth;

- He [**Adonai**] will judge between the nations and arbitrate for many peoples. Then they will hammer their swords into plow-blades and their spears into pruning-knives; nations will not raise swords at each other, and they will no longer learn war. And the L-RD G-d will be king over all the earth; in that day, He will be the only one, and His name [**Adonai**] the only one;

- Then **Adonai** will be king over the whole world. On that day **Adonai** will be the only one, and his name will be the only name.

Does that mean that we Jews believe that Mashiach is Adonai our G-d?

In order to reach this simple conclusion, that these verses truly are prophecies of Mashiach, then one must acknowledge that these prophecies describe G-d in the flesh, and that we look forward to Him fulfilling His word in person, here on Earth.

Mashiach

When we consider the specific prophecies, we find that they only occur after G-d makes a covenant of peace with Isra'el. Isra'el cannot be at peace with G-d until the sin that separates us from Him has been addressed. In light of these facts, the concept of a second coming of Mashiach is the only means of reconciliation between G-d and Isra'el. Once G-d brings Isra'el to national salvation then He will:

- Finish gathering the Jews back to our Land
- Establish His sanctuary in our midst
- Usher in an era of world peace
- Spread the universal knowledge of Himself

We await G-d's perfect timing for this event.

The exact phrase "second coming" is not found in either the Torah, the Tanakh or Brit Chadasha; but it is disingenuous to claim that no concept of the second coming exists in Scripture. If we believe there is only one "capital-M" Mashiach, then it is reasonable to think He would come twice because there are two distinct pictures of Him given in Scripture: the servant and the sovereign.

In Judaism the servant Mashiach is called Mashiach ben Yosef, in reference to the servant pictured by Joseph at the end of the book of Genesis. The book of Daniel refers to Mashiach being "cut off," and Joseph was cut off from his family. There are numerous parallels between Joseph and Mashiach. Judaism recognizes this.

The sovereign Mashiach is called Mashiach ben

D.A. Osterman

David in reference to the reigning sovereign pictured by King David. Numerous passages refer to the authority and kingdom of David, and yet David did not receive the fullness of those promises. Those promises find their fulfillment in the coming Mashiach and Judaism recognizes this as well.

Scripture provides a picture of this *return of the King*: "I will go and return to my place, till they admit their guilt and search for me, seeking me eagerly in their distress" (Hosea 5:15, CJB). Once the people of Isra'el acknowledge their guilt and seek His face, then Mashiach will return. That time will come, as G-d says:

> ...And I will pour out on the house of David and on those living in Yerushalayim a spirit of grace and prayer; and they will look to me, whom they pierced. They will mourn for him as one mourns for an only son; they will be in bitterness on his behalf like the bitterness for a firstborn son.   -- Zechariah 12:10 (CJB)

G-d provides evidence of a Second Coming. Is there other evidence?

Judaism recognizes "second comings." Every year at Passover, Jews all over the world look for the second coming of Elijah the prophet. At a specific point in the Seder meal, a child opens the door of the home and recites some words asking if Elijah has returned and inviting him into the home.

As Jews, will we finally accept that Mashiach has come to bring to us the salvation we crave? Will we

Mashiach

finally be at peace, and the Truth be seen by all? Before that happens, many people, both Jews and Christians, will deny Mashiach's second coming, including many who believe in the one True G-d.

As of today, only two of the requirements have been fulfilled or it is expected by most Jews to soon be completed: First, ingathering of the Jewish Exiles; and second, the rebuilding of the Holy Temple. At last count, 6.3 million Jews have already returned and are currently living in Isra'el. The rebuilding of the Temple could commence at any time.

Chapter 11
2 of 6? - What Does That Mean?

Two of the six requirements have or soon will be fulfilled. How can that be? Is our Mashiach here now, but we just don't know it? Are the six requirements correct? Did Mashiach appear but then leave us only to return at some future date? Or did we Jews just miss something? The literal answer to these questions is the fact today that one of the six requirements has already been met, and most Isra'elites agree a second requirement will be fulfilled soon as follows:

1. With the creation of the State of Isra'el, the ingathering of Jews back to the homeland has already commenced with almost one-half of the global Jewish population now living in Isra'el and more arriving every day.

2. Most agree that the third Temple will begin construction in the near future.

Mashiach

However, that means four have not been met and no one knows when to expect their fulfillment, except to say that these four will only occur after the appearance of Mashiach. But that goes right back to the first question above; How can that be? It certainly appears as though Mashiach did appear, and that he will return again to complete the four other prophesies. But as Jews, almost all of us would still argue that Mashiach only comes once and there is no such thing as a Second Coming of Mashiach as the Messianic Jews and Christians claim.

As uncomfortable as it is, something we need to look at and consider is the possibility that we are in a state of spiritual blindness. Spiritual blindness refers to our inability to comprehend spiritual truth, specifically failure to recognize the true identity of Mashiach. The prophet Isaiah discussed this in Isaiah 29 in the following verses:

If you make yourselves stupid, you will stay stupid! If you blind yourselves, you will stay blind! You are drunk, but not from wine; you are staggering, but not from strong liquor.

For Adonai has poured over you a spirit of lethargy; he has closed your eyes (that is, the prophets) and covered your heads (that is, the seers).

For you this whole prophetic vision has

become like the message in a sealed-up scroll. When one gives it to someone who can read and says, "Please read this," he answers, "I can't, because it's sealed." If the scroll is given to someone who can't read with the request, "Please read this," he says, "I can't read."

Then Adonai said: "Because these people approach me with empty words, and the honor they bestow on me is mere lip-service; while in fact they have distanced their hearts from me, and their 'fear of me' is just a mitzvah of human origin — therefore, I will have to keep shocking these people with astounding and amazing things, until the 'wisdom' of their 'wise ones' vanishes, and the 'discernment' of their 'discerning ones' is hidden away."

-- Isaiah 29: 9-14 (CJB)

Isaiah portrays his frustration with our Jewish ancestors who were at that time *not* led by G-d's Spirit, but by the world. This is a very similar situation to today's society. The more Isaiah speaks the truth, the less the Jews comprehended what he was describing. He attempted to point out that G-d is the one who allows us to hear his voice. However, if we continued to rebel against Him, he will withdraw his grace from the Jewish people.

The prophets and seers of his day had the technical skills to understand G-d's Word, but they lacked the spiritual insight to see the true meaning. And the situation for the common person was impossible. Today, it is much the same. Our fellow common Jews are far from G-d and in a place spiritually where they cannot see the truth.

It appears as though even Maimonides, never mind the common person and average Rabbi today, most likely missed the truth. If one reads Maimonides acclaimed writings on Jewish law and ethics with an open mind, it becomes easy to see that both Maimonides and today's Tanakh scholars are not studying messianic prophecy so as to determine what the Tanakh *actually says* about Mashiach as much as they are *studying it* so as to find a reason to deny Mashiach. How do we expect to answer the ultimate question we will be required to answer when we come before the judgment seat: "Did you crave the coming of the Mashiach?" We can't answer that question in the positive when we are only *looking* for ways to avoid *looking* for him and *looking* to deny Mashiach.

How did this happen to us?

Jewish weekly readings in the Synagogue were changed decades ago. As an example; the Reform Judaism and its split-off Reconstructionist Judaism generally do not accept the idea that there is a Mashiach at all. Some believe that there may be some sort of "messianic age" (the World to Come) in the sense of a "utopia", which all Jews are obligated to work towards. This became their official position regarding Mashiach when the 1885 Pittsburgh Platform rejected the traditional Jewish hope for an heir of King David to arise when the world was ready to acknowledge that heir as the anointed one. In the Avot, the first prayer of the Amidah, Reformers changed the prayer book's hope for a go-el, a redeemer, to geulah, redemption.

The first century Dead Sea Scrolls describe how the majority of Second Temple texts were changed to have no reference to an individual end-time Messiah and also removed the messianic prophecies which they believed were fulfilled already. And they altered words and definitions pointing to Yeshua. They made these changes for several reasons. Huge numbers of Jews were turning away from traditional teachings because of the prophecies described by Isaiah. Over the past two millennia, our expectations for Mashiach have changed, and Jewish leaders and scholars have devalued the depiction of many of the Mashiach passages.

Modern scholars, like Rabbi Tovia Singer as well as Rashi (Rabenu Shlomo Yitzchaki) (1040–1105 C.E.) and Origen (184/185 – 253/254 C.E.), view the *suffering servant* as a reference to the whole Jewish people, regarded as one individual, and more specifically to the Jewish people deported to Babylon. However, in aggadic (a compendium of rabbinic texts that incorporates folklore, historical anecdotes, moral exhortations, and practical advice in various spheres, from business to medicine) midrash on the books of Samuel, there is a statement that Isaiah 53:5 is messianically interpreted.

Today, in several Jewish circles there is a realization of the aggadic midrash, and ongoing discussion about a rapidly growing phenomenon called: Messianic Judaism. What is Messianic Judaism?

Mashiach

Messianic Jews are those Jews who believe that Mashiach promised in the Tanakh has already come as the *Suffering Servant*. He is the one that Messianic Judaism calls Yeshua.

Where did the first Messianic Jews come from? Beginning in the first century, Messianic Jews were considered just another movement within the Jewish religion, originating from the Jewish Essene movement. Today the differences between the various Jewish movements have mainly to do with the prayer services and related customs, and how the authority of the Torah is viewed.

While the Rabbis and Jewish leaders of today may have strong political convictions, neither they nor the Synagogue have very little direct involvement in our secular government and politics. During the first century, the Pharisees, Sadducees and even the chief priests were more interested in political power than religious correctness which was surely not G-d's will. Only the Essenes were solely focused on the Torah, and G-d, and the arrival of Mashiach.

However, the most important group of Jews over and above these organized movements (the Pharisees, Sadducees, or Essenes) were just plain Jews. Plain simple folk, who were at that time not led by G-d's Spirit, but by the world, a very similar situation to today's secular society. In varying degrees they lived their Jewish lives by following the ways that they had always done, whatever their mother and father taught them. Exactly like many Jews still do today as well.

There were a few of these average first century

Jews who observed the Sabbath, observed the holidays, observed the festivals, went on pilgrimages to the temple, and observed the Jewish food laws, and Jewish rituals, most were just plain secular citizens, born in Isra'el from Jewish parents. These plain folk believed in YHWH, following the ways by which to make their lives holy. They followed the dictates of the Torah. Many of these, if not most, were the ones mentioned by Josephus to be Messianic Jews. While there is no discussion of them in the Tanakh, we get a glimpse of some of them in the pages of the Brit Chadasha.

But how many people was Josephus actually talking about? There is no way of testing the numbers, but if the numbers are like any other kind of guess work done by a modern newspaper or an ancient historian, they're not absolute. Josephus mentions numbers like 6,000 Pharisees, 4,000 Essenes. Maybe there were 20,000 Priests. Of those Priests, how many were aristocrats and therefore Sadducees? No one knows, but I propose a fraction of that. So those numbers don't give us a very good account of the general Jewish common folk. Most historians and archeologists today agree there were around a million Jews during this juncture in antiquity, which means that most people belonged to none of the formal movements. Who were these people? What did they think?

We know very little about all these groups because we only have the evidence for the people who have articulated their ideologies. It certainly isn't out of line to assume that most Jews who did not associate with a group led what they thought was the correct Jewish life according to how they, or their local rabbi, interpreted

Mashiach

the Torah and Tanakh. This is the time when a large number were beginning to believe in what we now call Messianic Judaism. They were simple Jewish folk, and their numbers were growing. And because of that increase in number, the powerful Pharisees were becoming agitated. They were beginning to lose power with the growth of the Messianic Jewish movement. They were also losing influence, money, and status. *Lose a following and a religion dies.* They couldn't have so many people leaving the faith! They had to do something! They were like Temple dictators, always studying the Law, interpreting the G-d's Law, enforcing the Law, and influencing the Roman rules and rulers of the day. How? How could they get away with altering G-d's word?

The Pharisees were at various times a political party, a social movement, and a school of thought, especially during the Second Temple period, beginning under the Hasmonean dynasty (140–37 B.C.E.) in the wake of the Maccabean Revolt. The Pharisees were the sect that created oral traditions, put forth as being equal in authority to the written Word of G-d. As if any human could compare to the authority of G-d and His own Words! They used their power while they still enjoyed some level of popularity within the general population. As a defense mechanism they began to disparage the Messianic Jews, claiming they were practicing a false religion. In their effort to cling to power, they knew they had to eliminate the Messianic Jewish movement and the people who they believed were taking power away from them. Their attempts worked, with twisting words and their meanings, and exacting punishments, and making public all excommunications.

As followers of "The Way"—Yeshua—grew, however, it soon became impossible for a Messianic Jew to keep his Jewish identity. Upon being discovered, Messianic Jews were immediately cast out of the synagogues and the Temple into a religious "no-man's land." At that point in history, the Temple and the Synagogues were the very center of ALL society. Being "excommunicated" meant being forbidden from participating in virtually every single part of society. If one was excommunicated, your family was doomed. To be put out of the synagogue was a very grave issue. Being excommunicated meant you were outside of the community and without contact with G-d's people. Furthermore, because excommunication involved exclusion from the Jewish sacred assemblies, it automatically entailed a loss of access to the ritual sacrifices associated with divine forgiveness, and acceptance at the Temple and the Synagogues. They had no place to worship.

Then there were the Sadducees who preserved the authority of the written word of G-d, particularly the books of the Torah. At the time when Yeshua was alive, the Sadducees were more concerned with politics than religion. They were apathetic about Yeshua, until they became afraid He might bring unwanted Roman attention to Isra'el and the Jewish people. It was at this point that the Sadducees and Pharisees united and conspired to have the Romans put Yeshua to death. The Sadducees ceased to exist in 70 C.E. Since their

Mashiach

existence was dependent on political and priestly ties, when Rome sacked Jerusalem and destroyed the Second Holy Temple, the Sadducees ceased to exist along with the Temple.

The rejection of the Messianic Jewish movement as a legitimate sect of the Jewish faith continued for 1900 years. Finally in 1967, the situation began to change in parallel with Jerusalem coming under Jewish control. As we all know, In June, 1967, there was a short, violent Six-Day War between Isra'el and the Arab nations. Isra'el prevailed, and captured the old city of Jerusalem along with other territory.

Today, most Isra'elis are unaware that there is a small but thriving community of Messianic Jews in Isra'el. There are no hard numbers, but there are thought to be approximately 10-20,000 Messianic Jews living in Isra'el. Isra'elis who are aware of them in their midst—and think that it matters and they have to do something about it—tend to be Orthodox and ultra-Orthodox.

Messianic Jews in Isra'el say they are denied religious freedom. For example, under Isra'eli law they cannot immigrate there even if they are considered Jewish under the Law of Return, if the government determines that they've changed their religion to Messianic Judaism.

But that may be beginning to change. The Times of Isra'el recently ran a story under the headline: "Has the time come to accept Messianic Jews?" Isra'el is a small country—about the size of New Jersey—so the few congregations that exist do provide an opportunity for fellow Isra'elis to explore Messianic Judaism. Isra'el is beginning to be aware that there are Jews who believe Yeshua is the long awaited Mashiach, much as they did in the first century era.

The perception of Messianic Jews is undergoing a steady transformation in Isra'el these days—from one of mistrust and outright loathing to recognition and acceptance. With Jerusalem finally under Jewish control after 1900 years, several events prophesied in the Tanakh are beginning to occur. The appearance of Mashiach ben David is destined to appear soon, and He will bring about triumph for the Jewish people and the Nation of Isra'el and "Rule and Reign" from Jerusalem.

Although misunderstood, the six premises of Mashiach discussed in this book do reflect accurate messianic prophecies. Now there are only two questions left to address:

1. We don't know what the timing is for the appearance of Mashiach, and;
2. Whether Mashiach comes just once as the modernists believe, or twice as our ancient ancestors believed.

Mashiach

Yeshua

Ha-Notzri

Chapter 12
Are We Really Blind?

For two millennia, the rabbinical community has been considering, wondering and pondering how to solve the differences between the two Mashiach shown in the various prophecies in the Tanakh. First, the "Suffering Servant" prophecy that Mashiach will be rejected despised and killed, and then come again to bring Isra'el its long awaited "Rule and Reign" king. But most Jews today would simply state: "That's just not what a Jew believes."

In studying the prophecies about Mashiach in Isaiah Chapter 29, particularly Isaiah 29:9-14 as shown above, one will begin to think about the question that is the title of this chapter: "Are We Really Blind?" If so, then it is one of the saddest prophecies in the entire Bible. The story of us Jews rejecting our own Mashiach! After spending millennia desperately waiting and anticipating His arrival, did we just simply not recognize Him?

For 1,900 years, Christians and the few remaining

Mashiach

Messianic Jews have been trying to convince us Jews to accept their belief of a single Mashiach, Yeshua, who has already come once and will return. We Jews have resisted that belief. Accepting the conclusion that Yeshua was truly Mashiach and forgoing our long-held beliefs is a difficult change to bear. Indeed, most Jews today reject Yeshua a-priori, holding onto the idea that Mashiach is yet to come while Christians as well as a growing number of Messianic Jews believe that many of the major prophesies will only be fulfilled in a Second Coming.

Even more unfortunate, many Jewish people today have lost the hope of Mashiach altogether. For those still clinging to this belief, there is confusion and misunderstanding of the identification and purpose of Mashiach.

Judaism certainly doesn't exclude second comings per se. Quite the contrary. Every year at Passover, Jews all over the world look for the second coming of Elijah the prophet. At a specific point in the Seder meal, a child opens the door of the home and recites the words asking if Elijah has returned and inviting him into the home.

It is only because of **tradition** that we have been taught that Jews should not believe in Yeshua. The problem is, tradition is not always correct, valid, or in our best interest. Yeshua was a Jew. Both His parents were Jews. He was given a Jewish name at birth: Yeshua. It is important to stop here and say, that for those who have already made up their minds that Yeshua is not the Messiah, no amount of evidence will be convincing. But for those with open minds, who are honest in their asking and reading, the evidence truly speaks for itself.

To anyone who actually gives real consideration to the prophecies in the Tanakh of Mashiach, there is an absolutely amazing "Ah-ha" moment and revealing epiphany. For those of us who were previously blind, this awakening of knowledge and personal acceptance of Yeshua as Mashiach is a most rewarding and life-altering experience. Eyes widen with excitement and broad smiles beam on faces. "Wow! I get it!"

Suddenly, there is an understanding of what G-d was saying those many centuries ago when he told Moses, the Prophets, and the scribes of the Tanakh what to write. As they read and understand the powerful Messianic prophecies like Isaiah 53 and Jeremiah 31:31-33, one can almost literally feel and see the scales fall off of their eyes. Their response is always the same, as they ask, often with tears in their eyes, "Why didn't anyone ever show me this before?"

The Jewish belief in the coming of Mashiach was described by Joseph Klausner in his book, *Messianic Idea in Isra'el* (Machmillian, 1955), as "The most glistening jewel in the glorious crown of Judaism." Our Jewish faith in Mashiach sustained us through our long and torturous march through history as Klausner says below:

> I believe with a perfect faith in the coming of Mashiach, and though he tarries, I will wait daily for his coming.

Mashiach

This proclamation recited by Jews all over the world in daily prayers underscores the importance of the Mashiach concept.

Today Christians and Jews are coming together to love and support the majestic and humane Jewish state. At the same time, they are beginning to rediscover the deep Jewishness and religious commitment of Yeshua, a lost Jewish son who fought Roman paganism and oppression and was killed for it.

Yeshua was a wholly observant Pharisaic Rabbi who never claimed to abrogate the Torah but who observed every letter of the Law given by Moses. There is comfort in tracing most of Yeshua's teachings back to sources in the Torah and Tanakh. It is time as Jews to acknowledge Yeshua as a Jewish patriot. It is time we see him as the incredible Jewish teacher and the true rabbi he was.

Paula Fredriksen, in her book, *From Jesus to Christ*, has suggested that Yeshua's impact on his followers was so great that they could not accept the failure implicit in his death. Yet, Yeshua's resurrection can be proved with at least as much certainty as any universally believed and well-documented event in ancient history. Blaise Pascal, a French mathematician, physicist, and religious philosopher who laid the foundation for the modern theory of probabilities and statistics gives us simple, sound, and psychological proof of Yeshua's resurrection as follows:

> The apostles were either deceived or deceivers. Either supposition is difficult, for it

is not possible to imagine that a man has risen from the dead. While Jesus was with them, he could sustain them; but afterwards, if he did not appear to them, who did make them act? The hypothesis that the Apostles were knaves is quite absurd. Follow it out to the end, and imagine these twelve men meeting after Jesus' death and conspiring to say that he has risen from the dead. This means attacking all the powers that be. The human heart is singularly susceptible to fickleness, to change, to promises, to bribery. One of them had only to deny his story under these inducements, or still more because of possible imprisonment, tortures and death, and they would all have been lost. Follow that out. (Pascal, Pensees 322, 310)

Several very important factors are often overlooked when considering Yeshua's post-resurrection appearances to individuals. The first is the large number of witnesses of Yeshua after his resurrection. The Brit Chadasha records Yeshua appeared on 12 separate occasions to different group sizes ranging from just one person to over 500 people after his crucifixion and resurrection.

Another factor crucial to interpreting Yeshua's post-resurrection appearances is that He also appeared to those who were hostile or unconvinced. Many of us Jews have claimed that Yeshua was seen alive after His death and burial only by His friends and followers. Using that argument, we attempt to water down the overwhelming impact of the multiple eyewitness accounts. But that weak line of reasoning hardly deserves comment. As a perfect example, no informed individual would regard Saul of Tarsus as being a follower of Yeshua. The facts show the exact opposite. Saul despised Yeshua and persecuted Yeshua's followers of "The Way." It was a life-shattering experience when Yeshua appeared to him! Although he hated the disciples of Yeshua, he later becomes one: the apostle Paul, one of the greatest witnesses for the truth of the resurrection.

Shortly after his encounter with the resurrected Yeshua, Saul discusses the fact in the Brit Chadasha, that he saw the resurrected Yeshua as a glorified man. Saul makes the point of the light being seen. Yeshua says he appeared before Saul, revealed himself to him much like G-d did with Moses in the Torah. Here is Paul's (the name Saul took after his meeting of Yeshua) report about the meeting of the 500 in 1 Corinthians as follows:

> Now, brothers, I must remind you of the Good News which I proclaimed to you, and which you received, and on which you have taken your stand, and by which you are being saved — provided you keep holding fast to the message I proclaimed to you. For if you don't, your trust will have been in vain. For among the first things I passed on to you was what I also received, namely this: the Mashiach died for our sins, in accordance with what the

Tanakh says; and he was buried; and he was
raised on the third day, in accordance with
what the Tanakh says; and he was seen by
Kefa, then by the Twelve; and afterwards he
was seen by more than five hundred brothers
at one time, the majority of whom are still
alive, though some have died. Later he was
seen by Ya'akov, then by all the emissaries;
and last of all he was seen by me, even though
I was born at the wrong time. For I am the
least of all the emissaries, unfit to be called an
emissary, because I persecuted the Messianic
Community of G-d. But by G-d's grace I am
what I am, and his grace towards me was not
in vain; on the contrary, I have worked harder
than all of them, although it was not I but the
grace of G-d with me.
-- 1 Corinthians 15:1-10 (CJB)

The apostle is appealing to his audience's
knowledge of the fact that Yeshua had been seen by
more than 500 people at once. Paul reminds skeptics
that the majority of those people are still living
witnesses of Yeshua, and can be questioned. Dr. Edwin
M. Yamauchi, associate professor of history at Miami
University in Oxford, Ohio, emphasizes: "What gives a
special authority to the list above (of witnesses) as
historical evidence is the fact that most of the five
hundred witnesses were still alive. Paul says in effect,
If you do not believe me, you can ask them. Such a
statement in an admittedly genuine letter written within
thirty years of the event is almost as strong evidence as

Mashiach

one could hope to get for something that happened nearly two thousand years ago." Let us take the more than 500 witnesses who saw Yeshua alive after His death and burial, and place them in a courtroom. Do you realize that if each of those 500 people were to testify for only six minutes, including cross-examination, it would take an amazing 2+ days of NON-STOP testimony on the stand, 50 hours of firsthand testimony? Add to this the testimony the many other eyewitnesses, and you would have the largest and most lopsided trial in history.

But Isra'el's rejection of Yeshua and our spiritual blindness is just G-d's starting point in a process that will ultimately lead to faith in Yeshua as Mashiach, which then will result in unimaginable blessings both to Jews and to Gentiles. The rejection of Isra'el by G-d has never been total and final. Any time in the past when G-d turned away from His people, His back was to us only temporarily, even though this last turning away of G-d to us has lasted almost two thousand years. G-d is certainly not finished with his chosen people, in spite of our present unbelief in Yeshua. It is true we stumbled by our stubborn spurning of Yeshua. And we sought to establish our righteousness on the basis of our own works and not on the basis of grace that flows from the work of Yeshua. How can G-d's grace flow to us from Yeshua?

G-d has shown His limitless grace for His chosen people. Our sin and stubbornness can never stop G-d's plan to save His chosen people. In fact, G-d's grace only strengthens us. G-d's eternal plan to save us takes our sin into account. Yeshua died for the sins of *every* person, Jews and Gentiles. In fact, it was G-d's plan all along to save the Gentiles through us, the Jewish nation. But Isra'el failed to function as the light of the world. We made it difficult for the Gentiles to be saved. In fact we despised the Gentiles and called them dogs. Why? The first century Jews were proud of their privileges and work-righteousness, and they certainly didn't want to share that with the "Gentile dogs."

However, G-d had a plan, and used what could be called "reverse psychology" by encouraging the salvation of the Gentiles. In effect is was the same thing that G-d did when he used Cyrus the Great, a gentile, to rebuild the Second Temple around 538 BCE. With Yeshua, G-d planned to provoke the Jewish people to become envious in a positive sense. This plan of G-d's is clearly prophesied in the Torah:

> They aroused my jealousy with a non-god and provoked me with their vanities; I will arouse their jealousy with a non-people and provoke them with a vile nation.
> -- Deuteronomy 32:21 (CJB)

Jewish blindness to Mashiach, therefore, leads to Gentile salvation. Then Gentile salvation leads to positive envy of the Jewish people, and we are finally saved as a nation, which causes G-d to bless the Gentiles in an unparalleled and unimaginable fashion in the future.

Let's look closer at our whole area of darkness. This Spiritual Blindness is our inability to understand, perceive, grasp, and comprehend spiritual truth. A spiritually blind person is incapable of digesting, comprehending, perceiving the true meaning of G-d's spiritual truth.

The Tanakh speaks of blindness as a metaphor for spiritual ignorance, spiritual darkness, spiritual corruption, the inability to know G-d, or the inability to know the truth. That natural blindness, because of sin, is compounded by yetzer hara, our own evil inclination. That produces a kind of double-blindness. Our unbelieving minds are shut tight so that we cannot see through our eyes the light of Yeshua, the glory of who the Greeks call Christ, is truly the image of G-d. Thus our eyes and minds are blind. Even Nature knows this process. Light enters through the retina, pulses to the backs of our brains first and then our brains translate those impulses into what we see. But where Yeshua is concerned, we have become naturally blinded by our own yetzer hara.

When this blindness is continuous and remorseless, and when this blindness progresses, there is a third kind of blindness, a divine judgment blindness that brings about a fatal blindness. Isaiah prophesied in Isaiah 44:18 (CJB): "Such people know nothing, understand nothing. Their eyes are sealed shut, so that they can't see; their hearts too, so they can't understand." Why? G-d simply said the following in Isaiah:

Make the heart of this people [sluggish with] fat, stop up their ears, and shut their eyes. Otherwise, seeing with their eyes, and hearing

with their ears, then understanding with their
hearts, they might repent and be healed!
-- Isaiah 6:10 (CJB)

That's exactly what G-d told Isaiah in his vision.
They will hear and yet not understand. They will see
and yet not perceive. They will not believe, because
they have been hardened as a judgment by G-d.

Those of us who persist in unbelief cannot believe,
because, to paraphrase what was told to Isaiah by G-d:
"He blinded our eyes, hardened our hearts so we
couldn't see, perceive, and be healed." At that point,
blinded by G-d, we couldn't see, we couldn't perceive,
and therefore we cannot be saved. Yeshua's disciple,
Paul, wrote of such a judgment in the Brit Chadasha
book of Romans 11:8: "G-d has given them a spirit of
dullness—eyes that do not see and ears that do not hear,
right down to the present day." This is a dangerous
reality. This blindness is damning. Compounded
yetzer hara blindness is considerably more damning.
Terminal blindness, a judgment of G-d, could be the
removal of all hope.

Repeating the quote from Isaiah 29:9-14, G-d's
prophetic book dating to 740 B.C.E., Isaiah foretold
that G-d's own people will be blind to Mashiach
because they: "Distanced their hearts from G-d." The
majority of Jews, particularly the Rabbi's and biblical
scholars, don't want to heed Isaiah's words as follows:

If you make yourselves stupid, you will stay
stupid! If you blind yourselves, you will stay
blind! You are drunk, but not from wine; you

Mashiach

are staggering, but not from strong liquor. For Adonai has poured over you a spirit of lethargy; **he has closed your eyes** (that is, the prophets) and covered your heads (that is, the seers). For you this whole prophetic vision has become like the message in a sealed-up scroll. When one gives it to someone who can read and says, "Please read this," he answers, "I can't, because it's sealed." If the scroll is given to someone who can't read with the request, "Please read this," he says, "I can't read." Then Adonai said: "Because these people approach me with empty words, and the honor they bestow on me is mere lip-service; while in fact they have distanced their hearts from me, and their 'fear of me' is just a mitzvah of human origin — therefore, **I will have to keep shocking these people with astounding and amazing things, until the 'wisdom' of their 'wise ones' vanishes, and the 'discernment' of their 'discerning ones' is hidden away."** Therefore, here are the words of Adonai, who redeemed Avraham, concerning the house of Ya'akov: "Ya'akov will no longer be ashamed, no longer will his face grow pale. When his descendants see the work of my hands among them, they will consecrate my name. Yes, they will consecrate the Holy one of Ya'akov and stand in awe of the G-d of Isra'el. Those whose spirits stray will come to understand, and those

who complain will learn their lesson.
-- Isaiah 29: 9-14 and 22-24 (CJB)

According to the Tanakh books of Proverbs and Ecclesiastes, sinners walk in the ways of darkness. According to Isaiah 5:20, they substitute light for darkness and darkness for light. Why? They distance their hearts from G-d. What is the simple remedy for this type of blindness? According to Isaiah, we must draw close to G-d. How?

Blindness and darkness are metaphors for our condition as sinners. What this really means is that the whole world is full of people who engage in the nonproductive works of darkness, because they are part of the realm of darkness.

In the Tanakh when G-d begins to talk about Mashiach, He talks about Mashiach coming to bring us light: Isaiah 9, Isaiah 29, Isaiah 42, and Isaiah Chapter 60. In each of these references, Mashiach is seen as the one who brings spiritual light to the world in the midst of darkness. A light will shine when Mashiach comes. And as the Brit Chadasha book of John opens up, we hear:

> In the beginning was the Word, and the Word was with G-d, and the Word was G-d. He was with G-d in the beginning. All things came to be through him, and without him nothing made had being. In him was life, and the life was the **light** of mankind. The **light** shines in the darkness, and the darkness is not suppressed.
> -- John 1:1-5 (CJB)

Mashiach

Yeshua is **the light** of mankind.

Later in the Brit Chadasha book of John Chapter 8, Yeshua says: "I am the light of the world; whoever follows me will never walk in darkness but will have the light which gives life." And later again in John 12:46 Yeshua says: "I have come as a light into the world, so that everyone who trusts in me might not remain in the dark." In another book in the Brit Chadasha, Matthew Chapter 4: "The people who were sitting in darkness have seen a great Light. And those sitting in the land of the shadow of death upon them, a Light shined." That's Mashiach arriving to bring light to the darkness.

In the Tanakh, we discover Daniel, Chapter 7. Daniel is given a vision, and this vision occurs in the night as follows:

> I kept watching the night visions, when I saw, coming with the clouds of heaven, someone like a **son of man**. He approached the Ancient One and **was led into his presence**. To him was given rulership, glory and a kingdom, so that all peoples, nations and languages should serve him. His rulership is an eternal rulership that will not pass away; and his kingdom is one that will never be destroyed.
>
> -- Daniel 7:13 (CJB)

It is quite clear when we read this verse from the book of Daniel that the Son of Man clearly is **not** El-Elyon, the, "G-d most high." The Son of Man comes to El-Elyon. This is one to whom El-Elyon gives His eternal, everlasting universal kingdom. It is Mashiach, and He is the Son of Man, a prophecy that shows He will be incarnate. The Jews of Daniel's day all understood, "Son of Man," as a title for Mashiach.

How else can we overcome yetzer hara blindness? Spiritual blindness brings judgment. Tragic Judgment, now, and in the future. Spiritual blindness is completely unbending. The Pharisees who were constantly around Yeshua, and heard Yeshua tell these things to the crowds, said to Him, "We're not blind too, are we?" Metaphorically speaking, they all refused to admit their blindness. "We're not blind!" They said with disdain, arrogance, and scorn towards Yeshua. Paraphrasing their words: "You're not saying that we—the most learned, erudite, righteous, holy, virtuous, true representatives of G-d—are blind, are You?" Well, that's exactly what Yeshua was saying. The Pharisees thought they could see spiritually, which simply demonstrated they were spiritually blind. The idea of spiritual blindness to them was only a joke because they believed they were right with G-d, holy, and the absolute authority.

Spiritually blind people refuse to admit their blindness, and they finally reject "sight" when it's offered. In a discourse in the Brit Chadasha book of John 9:35-41, about a miracle Yeshua performs that gives sight to a lifelong blind beggar, Yeshua says to the Pharisees, "If you were blind, you would have no sin." Using a little play on words, consider the notion of blindness. However, Yeshua uses the term differently. In verse 40, He says, "You are blind," blind in the sense that you don't see your sin. But in verse 41, Yeshua says, "You're not blind." How is that? "If you were blind, you would have no sin." What does that mean? You are not blind to the truth. The truth is G-d's Torah. If you were blind to the truth, if you had no knowledge of the truth, no revelation of the truth; and if you didn't have the Scripture, the Tanakh, the laws of the Torah, all the prophets, and holy writings, then you wouldn't have me, Yeshua, here now. You wouldn't have all the demonstrations of who I am, because your sins would not be so severe. This would be like in times past, when G-d overlooked peoples' sins because His revelation was still incomplete. There was a lesser punishment, a less severe judgment on those who had no knowledge.

But we are not eyesight blind. We are just blind to our sins. We have been exposed to the truth. We know the truth because we read the truth daily in our prayers and during worship. We have the law, the prophets, the covenants, everything. The promises, the Tanakh. And as Yeshua told the Pharisees, (paraphrasing): "You've had Me. You've heard My words. You've seen the miracles. You have no excuse. Yes, blind to your own sin; but no, you are not blind to the truth."

Spiritual blindness receives judgment, refuses to admit its blindness, and rejects the offer of light and sight when it's given. Yeshua offered light, but they rejected it even when He was in their midst. What light? The Kingdom of Heaven, which is eternal life through Yeshua. Finally, this blindness results in doom. "You're doomed," Yeshua told the Pharisees. You are accepting the condition you're in, of spiritual blindness, as spiritual sight. You are doomed. You are hopeless. If you think you can see, you're doomed. Amazing play on words. Your sin remains. Finality. So, even though the light shines in the darkness, the darkness cannot extinguish it. The darkness cannot put it out, but the darkness rejects it. No matter how intensely and intently people reject the light, the light is there. One cannot get rid of it. Yeshua came to His own, the Jewish people, yet His own received Him not. Yet he is in the world. He made the world. "But the world knew Him not." They were the religious elite, the Pharisees. They were in darkness.

This discussion offers all of us Jews today many challenges. We need to realize our own utter spiritual poverty, blindness, and need for Yeshua. We need to see the desperate condition of everyone who has not been illumined by Yeshua, the Light of the World. We need to go to G-d in prayer and ask Him to reveal the ways we are rejecting the evidence of Yeshua because of our own experiences or our faulty understanding of Mashiach Yeshua. We need to consider before G-d whether we fully understand G-d; or, as is the case in the modern world, whether we have the opposite tendency to think there are many ways to get to G-d and heaven when we pass away. We need to ask if there is really an objective truth. Are the Scriptures of the Tanakh clear and coherent? As we become enlightened, we are guided by ruach ha-kodesh at the Synagogue, at home, or at work. We can see again as a people!

Mashiach

But this blindness is not just for Jews. Every unbeliever, Christian or Jew, Muslim or Buddhist, Atheists or literally any unbeliever is blinded to Yeshua as Mashiach until the ruach ha-kodesh opens their eyes. We were all blinded before we were convicted by HaShem.

Our Blindness to Yeshua is a mysterious part of Adonai's plan. The Jewish people for the last 1900 years have been in a state of disobedience so that the mercy Yeshua showed to the Gentiles, which resulted in their salvation, will in turn ultimately result in the salvation of the Jewish people. Our being caught in a state of disobedience is part of G-d's plan, so we will understand that we are not worthy of salvation, but that salvation only comes from His mercy and grace. Since we don't know G-d's exact timing, and since every soul is precious, we need to help all of Judaism understand the importance of Yeshua to all the Jewish people.

But what about the gentiles? How can they fit into our Biblical prophesies as they are apart from us? G-d worked out his eternal plan in history in spite of human sin and arrogance. He will do what only He knows is the perfect solution. Yeshua's apostles stressed to the Gentile majority not to be proud and not to despise the Jewish minority. Gentiles certainly have not replaced the Jews in G-d's plan as some have said (in error) in spite of the present unbelief of most Jews. Our hardening means only that Gentiles also are now included in G-d's plan. We might have excluded them, but G-d has not.

Finally, one of the largest barriers keeping Jews

from believing in Yeshua as Mashiach is the mistaken assumption that if a person believes in Yeshua, then he will no longer be Jewish. Nothing could be further from the truth. Messianic Jews are more Jewish than ever. Yeshua is Jewish, the Apostles are Jewish, the Brit Chadasha is Jewish. Believing Yeshua is Mashiach, the King of the Jews, is the most Jewish thing a person can do. Yeshua is the most Jewish of Jews! As we saw earlier in chapters 9 and 12, He is a descendant of King David. He was circumcised on the eighth day, spoke our language, lived in our Land, attended synagogue regularly, observed all of the Jewish customs, celebrated every Jewish holiday and kept all the laws of our Torah. He is Isra'el's Mashiach, our Chief Rabbi, our ultimate Prophet, High Priest and King.

In closing this chapter, some say that the Tanakh prophets did not seem to understand the distinction between the two comings of Yeshua (His coming at His birth in Bethlehem and His Second Coming) as seen in Isaiah 7:14; 9:6-7; and Zachariah 14:4. Those who argue that Yeshua was not the Mashiach because He did not fulfill all the Old Testament prophecies about the Mashiach in a 'Single' coming are simply denying the fact that while a second coming isn't specifically outlined in the Tanakh, a second coming isn't precluded either. They are blinded to the fact that all of these prophecies about Mashiach show that Yeshua's first coming was to stand in our place as a willing blood sacrifice offering and receive the penalty exacted by our Holy G-d for OUR sins. At His Second Coming, He will defeat all of G-d's and Isra'el's enemies. He will be the *Rule and Reign* king.

Don't let your pride blind you from the truth about Mashiach. The prophet Obadiah was always very succinct and wrote the shortest book in the Tanakh, he considered each word a high-priced commodity. In his vision he tells us in Obadiah 1:2-3 (CJB), Adonai Elohim told him: "Your proud heart has deceived you." Adonai also tells us in Prov. 29:23 (CJB) "The proud will be humbled..."

D.A. Osterman

Chapter 13
Yeshua is Mashiach - Is There Proof?

A cover story that first appeared in the April 2007 issue of *Isra'el Today* magazine discussed the fact that a few months before he died at the age of 108 on January 28, 2006, one of the Isra'el's most prominent rabbis, Yitzhak Kaduri was visited by Mashiach in a vision. In that vision Mashiach told Kaduri about himself, including His name. Shortly before his death Kaduri wrote what Adonai told him was the name of Mashiach on a small note and requested the envelope with the handwritten name remain sealed until one year after his death.

Kaduri was not only highly esteemed because of his age of 108. He was charismatic and wise, and devoted his life to Torah study and prayer on behalf of the Jewish people. The chief rabbis looked up to him as the Tzadik Ha-Dor. "Tzaddik" is a Hebrew term meaning, "a righteous one or saint." He would give advice and blessings to everyone who asked. Thousands visited him to ask for counsel or healing.

152

Mashiach

His followers speak of many miracles and his students say that he predicted many disasters.

When he died, more than 200,000 people joined the funeral procession on the streets of Jerusalem to pay their respects as he was taken to his final resting place. His funeral was attended by over 500,000 mourners and was described as the largest in Isra'el's history.

When the note he wrote was finally unsealed in April 2007, it revealed what many have known for centuries: Yehoshua, or Yeshua, is Mashiach. So was Kaduri the Tzadik Ha-Dor the priests had claimed, or was he just a "crazy old fool?" Most who were close to him knew there was nothing wrong with his mental faculties and acuity. They looked up to him as the "righteous one," Tzadik Ha-Dor.

Kaduri's unapologetic revelation confirmed what the prophet Malachi had predicted many centuries before as follows:

> But to you who fear my name, the sun of righteousness will rise with healing in its wings... -- Malachi 3:20 (CJB)

According to Jewish sages and tradition, this Sun of Righteousness referred to in Malachi's prophecy was understood to be Mashiach, who would have the power to heal whoever touched His tzit-tzit (fringes).

In addition to Rabbi Kaduri's vision, evidence to the belief in Yeshua as the true Jewish Mashiach is anchored in the "resurrection of the dead" a core Pharisaic doctrine. According to the Brit Chadasha,

Yeshua will return to usher in the Kingdom of G-d and fulfill the rest of Messianic prophecy such as the Resurrection of the Dead and the Last Judgment.

Now let's look at the innumerable Tanakh prophecies about Mashiach. Some people say these Mashiach prophesies are in the hundreds, and appear to be uniquely fulfilled in Yeshua. The possibility of these prophesies converging on any single ordinary man is completely ruled out by the laws of probability.

Of the many prophecies in the Tanakh, here is a list of what I consider the 10 most important:

1. Mashiach will be born in Bethlehem.
   Micah 5:2.
2. A massacre of children will happen at Messiah's birthplace — Jeremiah 31:15.
3. Mashiach will bring light to Galilee
   Isaiah 9:1-2.
4. Mashiach will be declared the Son of G-d
   Psalm 2:7.
5. Mashiach will be a sacrifice for sin.
   Isaiah 53:5-12.
6. Mashiach will be crucified with criminals.
   Isaiah 53:12.
7. Mashiach will resurrect from the dead.
   Psalm 16:10 & Psalm 49:15.
8. Mashiach will be seated at G-d's right hand.
   Psalm 68:18 & Psalm 110:1.
9. Mashiach will be called King.
   Psalm 2:6 & Zechariah 9:9.
10. G-d makes His "first-born the highest of the kings of the earth" - and – "rules over the

Mashiach

nations." — Psalm 89:19-29 & Psalm 22:27-31

Is there proof in these Tanakh prophecies that the true Mashiach must in fact be Yeshua?

That is certainly a difficult question. However, there are several interesting facts. Many of the prophecies in the Torah and Tanakh are framed by G-d to preclude their fulfillment by anyone living after the first century C.E. For example, the patriarch Jacob said in Genesis 49:10, "The scepter shall not depart from Judah, nor a lawgiver from between his feet, until Shiloh come." The name "Shiloh" is another title used for Mashiach, and the prophecy states that Judah's tribe will remain the chief tribe in Isra'el, until Mashiach comes. The prophecy must have been fulfilled prior to the destruction of Judah and Jerusalem in 70 C.E. The scepter certainly had departed from Judah by that point in history.

Further, as a Jew, it is very difficult to ignore the writings of the Brit Chadasha. For example, in the book of Matthew, which was written by a Jew for Jews, there are innumerable references to Mashiach prophecies that were fulfilled by Yeshua. Matthew cited Yeshua's virgin birth (Isaiah 7:14), the place of his birth in Bethlehem (Micah 5:2), the flight of his parents Mary and Joseph to Egypt to save him from Herod's massacre of all the male children (Hosea 11:1), the start of his preaching career in Galilee (Isaiah 9:1-2), the miraculous healings (Isaiah 35:5-6), being rejected by non-believers (Isaiah 53:3), his entrance into Jerusalem on a donkey (Zechariah 9:9), and his betrayal for thirty pieces of silver (Zechariah 11:12-13);, and finally, his painful prayers in the garden on the Mount of Olives. Then there is the illegal trial in the middle of the night, Yeshua's crucifixion, resulting in his burial and resurrection which are all described in Psalm 22 and Isaiah 53. And these are only a few of the fulfilled prophecies.

Similarly the covenant with King David that the Mashiach will be his descendant and reign as King eternal comes directly from G-d when He proclaims: "I will establish the throne of his kingdom forever" (II Samuel 7:13). Isaiah said, "There shall come forth a rod out of the stem (literally 'stump') of Jesse (that is David's father), and a Branch shall grow out of his roots" (Isaiah 11:1). "Jesse" is another name for Mashiach, and indicates that, even after it would appear that the family tree of Jesse has been cut down, yet one Branch will grow out of the stump. Evidently, the very last one "branch" emerging that could be known to have come from of this lineage would finally prove to be Yeshua, the promised Mashiach.

The "Jesse's Branch" prophecy was fulfilled uniquely in Yeshua. His foster father, Joseph, was in the royal line of David, and thus held the legal right to the throne (Matthew 1:1-16). His mother, Mary, was also a descendant of David, as shown by her genealogy in Luke 3:23-31. But since the time of Yeshua, it is quite impossible to establish the legal or biological descendant to lineage of any claimant to David's throne, as the entirety of the ancient genealogical records were destroyed during the destruction of the second Temple in 70 C.E.

Mashiach

An even more striking prophecy is given in Daniel 9:24-26. There Daniel was told explicitly that Mashiach would come as follows:

> Know, therefore, and discern that seven weeks [of years] will elapse between the issuing of the decree to restore and rebuild Yerushalayim until an anointed prince comes. It will remain built for sixty-two weeks [of years], with open spaces and moats; but these will be troubled times. Then, after the sixty-two weeks, Mashiach will be cut off and have nothing.
> -- Daniel 9:26-26 (CJB)

And the decree was given by the Persian emperor! Although the exact date of the decree is somewhat uncertain, the termination date of the prophecy by definition had to be some time in the first century C.E. In fact, the date was obviously before the destruction of the city and the temple by the Romans in 70 C.E., as the prophecy states quite explicitly that **Mashiach will be cut off**, but the people of a prince [Roman] shall come and destroy the city and the sanctuary. Not only must Mashiach come before this destruction, but He must also to be "cut off," which means, rejected and killed.

It is obvious that no one but Yeshua could have fulfilled these prophecies. The prophecies in the Torah and Tanakh absolutely preclude any appearance of a still future Mashiach, which if you are a believer in just a single coming of Mashiach, either means He already came, lived on Earth as the *Suffering Servant* and then went away, all without bringing about the prophesied Kingdom of G-d. It's either that, or G-d broke His covenant. So, does anyone really believe G-d broke His promise to his own chosen people? Or do we believe He will return once again in the future to fulfill the rest of the prophecies and establish the Kingdom of G-d here on Earth as promised?

G-d does not break promises and covenants:

> I am establishing my covenant between me and you, along with your descendants after you, generation after generation, as an **everlasting** covenant, to be G-d for you and for your descendants after you.
> -- Genesis 17:7 (CJB)

> From this you can know that Adonai your G-d is indeed G-d, **the faithful G-d, who keeps his covenant** and extends grace to those who love him and observe his mitzvot, to a thousand generations.
> -- Deuteronomy 7:9 (CJB)

If one entertains the thought that G-d has broken these promises and is an offender of his own laws, in either Judaic or Christian doctrines, then we are worshiping a deity, or object of worship, that is illegitimate in its professed authority and capability. Simply put, we are worshiping a false god.

If that is indeed true, then any of the claims made in the Bible concerning the existence of our G-d, any 'evidence' proposed by either Jewish or Christian

Mashiach

theists to support the Bible's various historical and supernatural claims, is absolute falsehood and essentially non-existent at best or manufactured at worst. Everything we have been taught about the biblical record from the creation of the universe to Adam and Eve, to Moses right up to the present has been a total waste of time; and in some cases, a total waste of an entire lifetime pursuing a falsehood. How Sad! However, parting with our faith and religion completely can be the only logical and obvious result.

But G-d's covenants are NOT fairytales, as any broken covenant would suggest. It's only because of a lack of faith we would say G-d could break his covenants. We limit our un-limitable G-d. Even if our rabbis put forth what they suggest is a pragmatic argument to support their own religious belief for why Yeshua cannot be Mashiach, their proposition in the end does not withstand close inspection and research to an embarrassment and richness of facts.

Many aspects of our religion require faith in us. Faith and trusting G-d even when it doesn't make any sense, even when we don't understand.

Still, many continue to be opposed to recognizing Yeshua as Mashiach. With all the evidence and the very specific and concrete prophecies in our Jewish Bible, throughout the Torah and Tanakh, that Yeshua fulfilled and thus proved He is Mashiach, the only conclusion left is that we are spiritually blind. And spiritual blindness is a very dangerous condition. Those who are spiritually blind do not know where they are going. They think they know, but they do not.

Chapter 14
The Brit Chadasha

The Brit Chadasha (New Covenant) is a Hebrew version of what Christians call the New Testament books. It presents a Messianic account of the life and times of Yeshua and his disciples with vocabulary that is consistent with present-day Jewish orthodoxy.

Jewish people who accept the Brit Chadasha and Yeshua as their personal Moshi'a (Savior) are able to study the Good News of the Brit Chadasha in a Jewish setting.

The traditional interpretation and approach to the Christian New Testament Scriptures has not taken sufficiently into account what it means to be Jewish. The Brit Chadasha Scriptures were written in the main by Jews, for Jews in a Jewish context.

The Complete Jewish Bible (CJB) referred to throughout this book, is a deliberately literal translation, word-for-word, even preserving the original idioms and verb tenses. The purpose of the literal approach is to preserve the text that the original Jewish authors intended.

This is not a version for the uninformed Gentile reader, as it requires at least a basic knowledge of Jewish history and tradition.

If the reader will forgive my generalization, there is within our Jewish character a certain combativeness. This character quality was developed as a result of the traditional yeshiva method of study, which was designed to be a mind-sharpening experience by its question and answer methodology.

For believers in The Way of Yeshua, this is a good thing. It brings to us an advantage resulting from the Jewish yeshiva method of training men of G-d. It allows those in the Messianic Jewish movement to learn and encounter in the Jewish manner of questions and challenges or objections to viewing both the Brit Chadasha and Yeshua.

Many Jews believe and claim that the Brit Chadasha generally follows the Christian King James translation as several of the available reference works come from and are based upon that version. However, as a Jew, if we examine all the evidence, most scholars today (even Christian Biblical Scholars) conclude that the Brit Chadasha was inspired in Hebrew and then later translated into Greek. Anyone studying these texts soon realizes that the Brit Chadasha is without a question Hebrew in grammar, idiom, and thinking. This opens up a whole new understanding of the essence of truth for the Brit Chadasha believer. If the Brit Chadasha is rooted in the Hebrew Language, then its teachings also derive from the Hebrew culture and are embedded in the Hebrew and certainly not a pagan Greek view of truth as many Jews have claimed over the centuries.

This one pivotal truth is being taught today, and real understanding of the Scriptures is breaking out everywhere! The true Hebrew Covenant of YHWH – everlasting life through Mashiach Yeshua, is at last being revealed.

> But he said, "Go your way, Dani'el; for these words are to remain secret and sealed until the time of the end. Many will purify, cleanse and refine themselves; but the wicked will keep on acting wickedly, and none of the wicked will understand. But those with discernment will understand.   -- Daniel 12:9-10 (CJB)

With G-d's revelations today, the secret mentioned by Daniel is finally being unveiled to the Jewish people. With these revelations, and the natural inquisitive mind of our Jewish people, every Jew will feel right at home reading the Brit Chadasha.

These books are best understood as a New Covenant with the Jewish people. As discussed, the word 'Brit' means "covenant" and 'Chadasha' means "new" in Hebrew. Like the Tanakh, it is typically divided into three parts: the Besorat HaGe'ulah or Gospels (corresponding to the Torah), Iggerot or Letters (corresponding to the Ketuvim), and Hitgallut or Revelation (corresponding to the Nevi'im).

This New Covenant was not unexpected by the prophets of the Tanakh. The original Messianic Jews,

Mashiach

and gentile believers in Yeshua as Mashiach (later called Christians) or followers of The Way, understood the Brit Chadasha truth as G-d intended, through the clarifying lens of Jewish practice and idiom that Mashiach had come to redeem Isra'el and reconcile all believers to G-d.

G-d promised this through his prophets Jeremiah and Ezekiel approximately 600 years before the appearance of Yeshua. Jeremiah promised that the Brit Chadasha would be even more gracious than the "Old Covenant" that G-d had made with Moses. Ezekiel added that G-d would also re-gather Isra'el, cleanse His people from all their filthiness, and give them a new heart and a new spirit.

But is the Brit Chadasha reliable? Because the Brit Chadasha provides the primary historical source for information on the resurrection of Yeshua, many Jewish critics have attacked the reliability of these documents.

Although there is overwhelming evidence that the Brit Chadasha is an accurate and trustworthy historical document, many people are still reluctant to believe what it says unless there is also some independent, non-biblical testimony that corroborates its statements. Some have gone so far as to claim that Yeshua is a completely made-up creation of the Jewish Zealots and Essenes.

However there is strong extra-biblical evidence that speaks directly about Yeshua as a real person.

The renowned Biblical modern day historian Edwin Yamauchi calls Tacitus "... probably the most important reference to Yeshua outside the New

Testament." Reporting on Emperor Nero's decision to blame the Christians for the fire that had destroyed Rome in A.D. 64, the Roman historian Tacitus wrote:

> Nero fastened the guilt . . . on a class hated for their abominations, called Christians by the populace. Christus, from whom the name had its origin, suffered the extreme penalty during the reign of Tiberius at the hands of . . . Pontius Pilatus, and a most mischievous superstition, thus checked for the moment, again broke out not only in Judaea, the first source of the evil, but even in Rome.

What this ancient document shows us is an unsympathetic reference to Yeshua and the early Christian movement. Tacitus provides an important written report showing that Christians derived their name from a historical person called Christus (from the Latin), or Christos (in Greek). He is said to have "suffered the extreme penalty," obviously alluding to the Roman method of execution known as crucifixion. This is said to have occurred during the reign of Tiberius and by a sentence of Pontius Pilatus. Confirming much of what the Brit Chadasha tell us about the death of Yeshua.

Another important extra-Biblical source about Yeshua and early Christianity is contained in the letters of Pliny the Younger to Roman Emperor Trajan. Pliny was the Roman governor of Bithynia in Asia Minor. In one of his letters, dated around 112 C.E., he asks Trajan's advice about the appropriate way to conduct

Mashiach

legal proceedings against those accused of being Christians. Pliny states he needs to consult with the emperor about this issue because by then a very large number of people of every age, class, and sex stood accused of Christianity.

At one point in his letter, Pliny relates some of the information he has learned about these Christians, as follows:

> They were in the habit of meeting on a certain fixed day before it was light, when they sang in alternate verses a hymn to Christ, as to a god, and bound themselves by a solemn oath, not to any wicked deeds, but never to commit any fraud, theft or adultery, never to falsify their word, nor deny a trust when they should be called upon to deliver it up; after which it was their custom to separate, and then reassemble to partake of food–but food of an ordinary and innocent kind.

Pliny states a number of revealing facts regarding the beliefs and practices of early Christians:

1. Christians regularly met on a certain fixed day for worship.
2. Their worship was directed to Christ, demonstrating that they firmly believed in His divinity.
3. Finally Pliny's statement that hymns were sung to Christ, as to a god, as a reference to

> the rather distinctive fact that, "unlike other gods who were worshipped, Christ was a person who had lived on earth."

Pliny understood that the first century Messianic Jews and Christians were worshipping an actual historical person as G-d. Pliny's statement correlates entirely with the Brit Chadasha doctrine that Yeshua was both G-d and man.

Another highly remarkable reference to Yeshua outside the Bible can be found in the writings of Josephus, the first century Jewish historian.

A Jewish priest, Josephus was an aristocrat in first-century Palestine and ended up living in Rome, supported by the patronage of three successive Roman emperors.

In Josephus two great works, *The Jewish War* and *Jewish Antiquities*, both written in Greek for educated people of the day , Josephus tries to appeal to aristocrats in the Roman world, presenting Judaism as a religion to be admired for its moral and philosophical depth. *The Jewish War* doesn't mention Yeshua, except in some versions in likely later additions by others. However, *Jewish Antiquities* does mention Yeshua—twice.

The shorter of these two references to Yeshua (in Book 20) is incidental to identifying Yeshua's brother James, the leader of the church in Jerusalem. In the temporary absence of a Roman governor between Festus's death and Albinus's arrival in 62 C.E., the high priest Ananus instigated James's execution. Josephus describes the execution and James as follows:

Mashiach

Being therefore this kind of person [i.e., a
heartless Sadducee], Ananus, thinking that he
had a favorable opportunity because Festus
had died and Albinus was still on his way,
called a meeting [literally, "Sanhedrin"] of
judges and brought into it the brother of
Yeshua-who-is-called-Mashiach … James by
name, and some others. He made the
accusation that they had transgressed the law,
and he handed them over to be stoned.

James is otherwise a barely noticed, minor figure in
Josephus's lengthy tome.   He identified James by
reference to his famous brother Yeshua. But James's
brother Yeshua also had a very common name.
Josephus mentions at least 12 other men named
Yeshua.   Therefore Josephus specified which Yeshua
he was referring to by adding the phrase "who is called
Mashiach," or, since he was writing in Greek, Christos.
This phrase was necessary to identify clearly first
Yeshua and then, through Yeshua, James, the subject
of the discussion.
   This extraneous reference to Yeshua would have
made no sense if Yeshua had not been a real person.
Thus, Yeshua did exist, and people were dying horrible
deaths rather than retracting their belief in Yeshua as
their G-d and Savior. They saw Yeshua, heard Him;
and some even experienced new life and healing
because of His touch. Yeshua resurrected people, and
made their minds and tortured spirits whole and normal.

D.A. Osterman

How could those healed and normal eye witnesses say lie and say they couldn't walk, see, hear, or touch their healed skin when they were so visibly changed?

Josephus' short identification of James by the title that some people used in order to specify Yeshua's brother gains credibility as an affirmation of Yeshua's existence *because* the passage is not about Yeshua. Rather, his name appears in a functional phrase that is called for by the sense of the passage. It can only be useful for the identification of James if it is a reference to a real person, namely, "Yeshua who is called Christ."

The longer passage in Josephus's *Jewish Antiquities* (Book 18) that refers to Yeshua is known as the Testimonium Flavianum.

Some skeptics of the Testimonium Flavianum have suggested that it is a forgery by Christians at some later date. In the quote below, the author has highlighted the parts that are thought suspicious because they sound Christian and many believe they were inserted decades after Josephus passing are in italics:

> Around this time there lived Jesus, a wise man, *if indeed one ought to call him a man.* For he was one who did surprising deeds, and a teacher of such people as accept the truth gladly. He won over many Jews and many of the Greeks. *He was the Messiah.* When Pilate, upon hearing him accused by men of the highest standing among us, had condemned him to be crucified, those who in the first place came to love him did not give up their affection for him, *for on the third day, he*

Mashiach

appeared to them restored to life. The prophets of G-d had prophesied this and countless other marvelous things about him. And the tribe of Christians, so called after him, have still to this day not died out.

Interestingly, all surviving manuscripts of the Testimonium Flavianum that are in Greek, like the original, contain the same version of this passage, with no significant differences, which is why there is uncertainty to the claim that Christians added to the original Josephus text - no one knows for sure.

We learn quite a bit about Yeshua from just these few famous historians; Tacitus, Pliny and Josephus, none of which were Christian. Almost all the following statements about Yeshua, which are asserted in the Brit Chadasha, are corroborated or confirmed by the relevant passages in Tacitus, Pliny and Josephus. These independent historical sources—non-Christian Roman as well as Jewish, confirm what we are told in the Brit Chadasha, called the Gospels:

1. He existed as a man. The historian Josephus grew up in a priestly family in first-century Palestine and wrote only a few decades after Yeshua's crucifixtion and death. Yeshua's known associates, such as Yeshua's brother James, were his contemporaries. The historical and cultural context was second nature to Josephus. As Robert Van Voorst observes:

D.A. Osterman

If any Jewish writer were ever in a position to know about the non-existence of Yeshua, it would have been Josephus. His implicit affirmation of the existence of Yeshua has been, and still is, the most significant obstacle for those who argue that the extra-Biblical evidence is not probative on this point. And Tacitus was careful enough not to report real executions of nonexistent people.

2. His personal name was Yeshua, as Josephus informs us.

3. He was called Christos in Greek, which is a translation of the Hebrew word Mashiach, both of which mean "anointed," or, "(the) anointed one," as Josephus states and Tacitus implies, unaware, by reporting, as Romans thought, that his name was Christus.

4. He had a brother named James (Jacob), as Josephus reports.

5. He won over both Jews and "Greeks" (i.e., Gentiles of Hellenistic culture), according to Josephus, although it is stretching the truth to say that they were "many" at the end of his life. Large growth in the number of Yeshua's actual followers came only after his death.

6. Jewish leaders of the day expressed unfavorable

opinions about him, at least according to some versions of the Testimonium Flavianum.

7. Pilate rendered the decision that he should be executed, as both Tacitus and Josephus state.

8. His execution was specifically by crucifixion, according to Josephus.

9. He was executed during Pontius Pilate's governorship over Judea (26–36 C.E.), as Josephus implies and Tacitus states, it was during Tiberius's reign.

As far as the author knows, no ancient person ever seriously argued that Yeshua did not exist. Referring to the first several centuries C.E., even a scholar as cautious and thorough as Robert Van Voorst freely observed:

> … no pagans and Jews who opposed Christianity denied Yeshua's historicity or even questioned it.

Non-denial of Yeshua's existence is particularly notable in rabbinic writings of the first several centuries C.E., if anyone in the ancient world had a reason to dislike the Christian faith, it was the rabbis. To argue successfully that Yeshua never existed but was a creation of early Christians would have been the most effective argument against Christianity. But all Jewish sources treated Yeshua as a fully historical person. Indeed, the rabbis used the real events of Yeshua's life against him.

Antiquities research by the end of the 19th century C.E., had confirmed the accuracy of the Brit Chadasha manuscripts. The research unveiled several early papyri documents which bridged the gap between the time of Yeshua and existing manuscripts from a later date.

All of these findings increased scholarly confidence in the reliability of the Brit Chadasha. William F. Albright, who during the 19th century was considered the world's foremost biblical archaeologist, said:

> We can already say emphatically that there is no longer any solid basis for dating any book of the Brit Chadasha after about A.D. 80, two full generations before the date between 130 C.E. and 150 C.E. given by Jewish critics of the Brit Chadasha today.

In addition to these papyri discoveries, we now have an additional 24,000-plus copies of other early manuscripts in existence today. Sir William Ramsay, a Scottish archeologist, was an atheist and the son of atheists. He tried to disprove the Bible for most of his career. He was considered the foremost authority of his day on the history of Asia Minor and a leading scholar in the study of the Brit Chadasha

Ramsay spent 15 years attempting to undermine Yeshua's disciple Luke's credentials as a historian, and to refute the reliability of the Brit Chadasha. He couldn't, and he finally concluded:

> Luke is a historian of the first rank … This author [Luke] should be placed along with the very greatest of historians.

Jewish biblical scholars are now pointing to important discoveries which serve to illuminate the very Hebrew style of speech used by Yeshua and his first followers, allowing for a more accurate translation of the Brit Chadasha. They have provided an increased understanding of the language that Yeshua spoke, enabling corrections of the numerous mistranslations in the English text of the Christian New Testament.

Hebrew University of Jerusalem Professor David Flusser, the world's leading Jewish authority on the Brit Chadasha as well as the early days of the gentile Christian church, is firmly convinced that the life of Yeshua was originally written entirely in Hebrew.

Dr. Moshe Bar-Asher, also of Hebrew University the leading Jewish scholar on the Aramaic language, agrees. He thinks the Brit Chadasha goes back to a Greek translation of an original Hebrew (not Aramaic) document.

In addition to these Isra'eli scholars many others around the world have reached this conclusion as well. The Norwegian Harris Birkeland declares that "The Language of the common people in Palestine in the time of Yeshua was Hebrew." William Sanford LaSor, professor emeritus of the Brit Chadasha at Fuller

Theological Seminary in Pasadena, California. (a renowned Semitic scholar) has said, "With the discovery of the Dead Sea Scrolls, it now seems highly probable that the language Yeshua spoke was Hebrew and not Aramaic."

Beside these reports and opinions, a large amount of evidence points to the use of Hebrew in first-century Isra'el: the testimony of the church fathers, the Dead Sea Scrolls, coins, and inscriptions from the first centuries B.C.E. and C.E., the large amount of writings by Josephus, as well as Rabbinic Literature of the day all point to Hebrew as the language of first century Jews.

Further confirming evidence that the Brit Chadasha was truly written by Jews for Jews can readily be seen in the written structure used by the scribes of the books.

Indeed, the writers of the Brit Chadasha quote the Hebrew Scriptures using the cultural mindset of the first century in which they lived.

The Brit Chadasha, because it is a Jewish book and written by Jewish authors, is very consistent in the way it uses the Hebrew Scriptures.

The Brit Chadasha is a continuation of YHWH's "G-d-breathed" mitzvot/words wherein we see many Tanakh prophecies unfold; especially the Mashiach prophecies outlined in Isaiah 53.

While the Torah contains the ONLY actual Words/Divine Instructions in Righteousness from YHWH himself as given directly to Moses, it is wrong to say that the Brit Chadasha is not divinely inspired. Without the Brit Chadasha, the plethora of evidence confirming many of the Tanakh's prophecies as well as

Mashiach

the detailed teachings about Yeshua and His ministry while He walked the earth would not exist. After all, Yeshua was "Immanuel" (G-d with us); our divine Mashiach who performed miracles and spoke many awesome things to teach YHWH's people how to live holy, set apart lives!

YHWH needed us to see "the whole picture." G-d starts His picture in the Torah book of Genesis and ends His picture-perfect plan with the Brit Chadasha book of Revelation. It is the rest of the story

With the preponderance of evidence from antiquity, starting with Josephus, right up to ongoing discoveries in the 21st Century confirming information laid out in the Brit Chadasha, we are reassured as to the accuracy of the Brit Chadasha. And from the accuracy of the Brit Chadasha, the accuracy of the Tanakh is established as well.

The author hopes you see how this small selection of ancient non-Christian sources helps corroborate our knowledge of Yeshua from the Brit Chadasha. Of course, there are many ancient Christian sources of information about Yeshua as well. But since the historical reliability of the canonical Brit Chadasha is so well established, I invite you to read it closely for a better view of the life of Yeshua.

Chapter 15
Arrival of Mashiach

Will there be a second coming of Mashiach Yeshua? Is Yeshua the true Jewish Mashiach we all have been waiting for? We have believed for centuries that our "Rule and Reign" Mashiach would be human; but as we have seen above, he also has a "Spiritual" component.

To answer the first question, since only two of the requirements have been (or soon will be) fulfilled of the six, we must continue to wait for the "second coming" before the other four components are fulfilled.

The second question has certainly been answered in Chapter 13. Yeshua was a Torah observant, tallit-wearing, Seventh Day Sabbath and Biblical Feast-keeping, kosher Jew! So that takes care of the Jewish part.

In spite of the facts pointed out in Chapter 13, particularly the fact that Mashiach could not be anyone after the first century C.E., most Jewish people still contend Yeshua was not the true Mashiach. The main objection to Yeshua lies in the truth surrounding his resurrection and the belief that the body of Yeshua was somehow stolen. Let's take a look at this stolen body hypothesis which posits that the body of Yeshua was stolen from his burial place. His tomb was found empty not because he was resurrected, but because the body had been hidden somewhere else by the apostles or some unknown persons, perhaps the original tomb owner.

This hypothesis has existed since the days of the first century Messianic Jewish movement. It is also discussed in the Brit Chadasha book of Matthew, which both Jewish and Christian experts agree was written between 70 and 100 C.E.

In the first book of the Brit Chadasha, Matthew raises this hypothesis of the stolen body only to refute it. He states the Jewish high priests spread that lie because they and the Pharisees knew the prophecy well and were fearful Yeshua would rise from the dead in three days. If true, the resurrection would prove without doubt that Yeshua was indeed Mashiach, and that would jeopardize their power and political standing.

However, when Yeshua was crucified, followed by his resurrection from the tomb three days later, the guards were left with an empty tomb, and the Temple elders were faced with a dilemma. They had to deal with not only an empty tomb, but also eyewitness accounts, from Yeshua's disciples and acquaintances to neutral witnesses of Yeshua's resurrection. What could they do? Three options were possible:

1. They could accept the testimony and believe in Yeshua whom they had crucified;
2. They could complain to Pilate about his incompetent soldiers; or,
3. They could enact a cover-up stating Yeshua's body was stolen.

The Sanhedrin and the Pharisees were not yet willing to accept Yeshua as Mashiach. If they complained to the Roman Governor Pilate, he would either believe them or slay the soldiers. If he believed them, the Jews would be defeated. If he slew them, the Jews would still be left with an inexplicably empty tomb. Yet, think about their first fear: the Jews would be defeated and conquered.

The Sanhedrin and the Pharisees had seen with their own eyes—facts and evidence—Yeshua raised Lazarus from the dead and other resurrections (Matthew 9:24; Matthew 10:8; Matthew 11:5; Luke 7:12-13; Luke 7:22); John 5:25; John 11:44; John 129; John 12:17; and, John 21:14). They saw Yeshua heal people and unite Romans, Jews, Greeks, and the worst-of-the-worst sinners.

To admit Yeshua was truly G-d, they would have to believe G-d would have a way to defeat Roman rule and reign. That's what they wanted a real Mashiach to do: to appear, to battle the Romans with the L-rd's Army, and to make Isra'el the ruling power in the world. Yeshua did not fulfill that expectation, so there was really only one option for them: a cover-up.

The Roman soldiers were greedy, and the Jewish

Mashiach

leaders paid them hush-money to convince them to cover up the truth. After all, they were in mortal danger anyway, and they hoped Pilate would also be amenable to bribery because Roman officials were indeed known to take bribes to render desired decisions. The Roman soldiers really had no other choice.

So the Jewish leaders paid off the soldiers to give a false report to Pilate. Their story was to be as follows: "The body of Yeshua was stolen from the tomb by his disciples." This would give the Sanhedrin and Pharisees ammunition to deny and then to persist in their claim that the disciples story of a resurrected Yeshua was pure fabrication and falsehood.

From that day forward, their false report circulated throughout Isra'el, Rome and every point in between. "The disciples had stolen Yeshua's body" became the official Jewish position on the resurrection of Yeshua. Several decades later, Tertullian (AD 160–225) acknowledged that this lie was still being used in his day as it is even today, almost 20 centuries later.

But can that story, or the other variations of the 'stolen body' stories, really hold water? Let's think about these varying stories logically. Here are a few of the variations of the stolen body story that have been put forth over the centuries:

The Romans stole the body? Romans had no motivation to steal Yeshua's body. He was just another of the hundreds of crucifixion victims that year. Besides, who would go against all those armed Roman guards at Yeshua's tomb? There's a fear factor at play here. No one had guns back then. Pilot put a solid wall of guards, in front of a giant stone, at Yeshua's grave as indicated in the following verses:

> You may have your guard, [Pontius Pilot tells the Head Priest and Pharisees]. Go and make the grave as secure as you know how.' So they went and made the grave secure by sealing the stone and putting the guard on watch -- Matthew 27:65-66 (CJB)

What would a Roman "guard" be? They were an elite recruitment of Roman soldiers, specially trained for battle. According to Matthew 28:11, there were more than two. Four men in a guard is in fact the minimum that protocol would dictate (see for example John 19:23), with each man taking a three-hour watch throughout the night.

When Yeshua's body suddenly disappeared from out of his tomb the next morning, the following event occurs. "Some...went into the city and reported to the head cohanim everything that had happened" (Matthew 28:11). For someone to make it through the barricade and roll back the gigantic stone and steal Yeshua's body would be impossible. The guards saw, and believed Yeshua had been resurrected; however, making money meant more than telling the truth, as Yeshua once said:

> Now the seed sown among thorns stands for someone who hears the message [truth about Yeshua being Mashiach], but it is choked by the worries of the world and the deceitful

Mashiach

glamor of wealth, so that it produces nothing.
-- Matthew 13:22 (CJB)

Could Joseph of Arimathea have stolen Yeshua's body? As information in the above paragraph explains, the Roman guard and the stone through which Joseph of Arimathea and his friends would have to fight through were impenetrable without an army equipped with fighting weapons. Joseph of Arimathea was no fighting man, and in no way could he and a few scrawny untrained friends have conquered those Roman guards let alone have the muscle to roll back a giant stone that was permanently sealed. Most likely with mortar. Furthermore, to touch a dead body or be in the vicinity of a buried body was considered unclean. You needed to be purified in the Temple if you'd touch a grave. No Jewish person would go near Yeshua's body for that reason alone yet to fight an entire Roman guard, and then use chisels to dislodge all that mortar that was hardening as a sealant.

Could Yeshua's disciples have stolen the body? This is the main argument even today used by the majority of Jews worldwide who deny Yeshua's resurrection. There are multiple problems with this claim that the disciples stole the body. First, why would these men even attempt such a feat? Immediately after the crucifixion they were on the run or in hiding (Mark 14:50) and didn't understand how Yeshua was to rise from the dead, "for as yet they did not know the Scripture, that He must rise again from the dead" (John 20:9; cf. Matthew 16:21–22; Luke 24:6–8; John 2:22).

Even though Yeshua had told them on multiple occasions that He would die and rise again, the disciples did not comprehend His words because they, like their fellow Jews in those days, expected Mashiach to usher in an unending Jewish political kingdom. That Mashiach would die was far from their expectations. So when Yeshua was crucified, the disciples were distraught and fearful.

Later, these same frightened and nervous disciples suddenly become fearless preachers of The Way. If their message was a sham, why would they be willing to leave their families alone without a means of support, endure continual persecution, imprisonments, and eventually martyrdom for a made up story? Liars don't make good martyrs! Wouldn't you recant a lie if someone threatened to kill you? All they had to say was, *Yeshua was not from G-d, was not our Mashiach, and only Caesar is King.* They didn't do that because they would then have to deny everything they experienced while living and visiting town-upon-town and healing with Yeshua, who had also given them divine powers to heal the infirmed themselves (Mark 6:12-13). Some people may be willing to die for a lie, but only if they believe it to be true. However, to think that a group of *twelve* men, with nothing to gain and likely everything to lose, would be willing to suffer and die for a fictional story strains credulity to the breaking point.

Could the Jewish elders have stolen Yeshua's body and then blamed other groups? The Jewish leaders knew of Yeshua's statements that he would be raised from the grave after three days, and were certainly

Mashiach

unsympathetic to Yeshua (Matthew 21:45-56 and Matthew 22 for examples), and so they would never steal his body. Indeed, they were the ones who insisted that a Roman guard (group of soldiers) be placed at the entrance to the tomb to prevent his body from being stolen. Not a trivial force to be reckoned with as mentioned above, indeed, while the minimum of four guards is used in the example above, a Roman guard could consist of as many as 16 fully-armed soldiers who were battle hardened. Furthermore, their duty assignment was on pain of their own death if they failed. Pontius Pilot ordered them to keep Yeshua's tomb secure, so they'd never subvert Pilot's order and steal the body themselves, even for money.

So back to the main argument still being used today, that the disciples stole Yeshua's body from the tomb. In order to make this claim and sound even halfway serious, you would need to dispute the Brit Chadasha account of the disciples fleeing in fear, which means that you claim that the disciples were bold and crafty enough to invent a false religion and preach it amidst opposition. And in addition that they were willing to die, sacrificing their own lives for a fictional made up story! Why then did they tolerate the accounts that portrayed them in such a poor light? And why would they accept Saul, a Pharisee and a total stranger, as G-d's messenger? Saul, whose name changed to Paul after his Damascus conversion, was someone who had persecuted, and delivered over for execution, *hundreds* of followers of Yeshua. He wanted all followers of "The Way" to renounce their belief in

Mashiach Yeshua and return to their Orthodox Jewish faith. Would the disciples really have believed Saul had greater insight than they themselves? They who had lived and traveled day-in and day-out with Yeshua and listened to his teaching for years? And why would they be willing to die rather than deny the resurrection? Again, these are questions concerning motive and motivation that have *no* answers because the Romans, Yeshua's disciples, and the Jewish elders had too much at stake to lose if any of these groups had stolen the body.

And there are more questions that have no answers because they make no sense. If the Jewish religious leaders or Romans suspected that Yeshua's disciples had stolen his body, why didn't they just interrogate them, or torture them? One could claim that they did, but there is no evidence confirming any such interrogation. After all, aren't we searching *right here* for evidence?

Since the Mashiach could not be anyone who lived after the first century C.E., combined with the logic surrounding the stolen body theories discussed above, the author must conclude that Yeshua is indeed the true Jewish Mashiach.

In spite of this, Jewish experts are still attempting to use history to disprove Yeshua and the resurrection. However, if you really look at the historical records, you will readily realize there is a lack of substance to support their position, and a large body of evidence verifying Yeshua's resurrection and divinity.

To those holding to their conviction that Yeshua's body was stolen, here is another question: Why even years later would these eleven men choose to continue with a lie only to be tortured to death (as most were) for a made-up cause and religion rather than reveal where the stolen body was hidden? It just doesn't make sense; the "Stolen Body Theory" fails at a basic level.

When all is said and done, all these false stories about Yeshua's body being stolen from a well-guarded tomb instead of G-d raising Yeshua from the dead suffer a fatal blow. There is no evidence. The only reason why such a theory would be accepted is because one does not want to accept the "embarrassment of riches" with regard to the evidence that Yeshua rose from the dead. But, other than that, there is no reason to even consider this theory.

In spite of this simple logic, the Temple elders and Pharisees of the day worked to spread this story of a stolen body. However, contrary to their desire, everywhere that false report traveled, so went one important fact—the tomb was empty! Just as it is reported in the Brit Chadasha:

> Then they met with the elders; and after discussing the matter, they gave the soldiers a sizeable sum of money and said to them, 'Tell people, His talmidim [Torah scholar versed in Jewish law] came during the night and stole his body while we were sleeping. If the governor hears of it, we will put things right with him and keep you from getting in trouble. The soldiers took the money and did as they were told, and this story has been spread about

D.A. Osterman

by Judeans till this very day.
-- Matthew 28:12-15 (CJB)

If Jewish authorities or anyone else they knew had the body in their possession or had knowledge of where it was, why didn't they, when the disciples were preaching the resurrection of Yeshua in Jerusalem, simply explain: "Wait! We (or they) moved the body. He didn't really rise from the grave." And if this simple verbal rebuttal failed, why didn't they disclose exactly where they had laid Yeshua's body to rest? And if that failed, couldn't they just go and recover Yeshua's body, and drag it through the center of Jerusalem? Put the body somewhere for everyone to find?

Again, the majority of us Jews are still spreading this tale (and accepting it) in the twenty-first century, unfortunately as fact.

In spite of the cover-up "story" promoted by the Sadducees and the Pharisees, Judaism of the first century was vibrant, exciting, diversified and spiritually alive. Had this not been the case, the Messianic Jewish and the gentile Christian Church would not have emerged. Indeed, much of that which is cherished in Christianity today is a by-product of the rich spirituality that is Judaism.

Then, as now, the difference between Jewish movements was not so much a matter of doctrine or theology, but how literally each individual movement accepted the scriptures. All twelve of Yeshua's Apostles were Jewish, including Paul, who was a former Pharisee. Yeshua's first directive to the

186

Mashiach

Apostles was to go tell the good news to "the lost sheep of Isra'el." Even Yeshua himself was at first reluctant to reveal the good news of the Gospel to a Canaanite woman who asked for his help. Yeshua finally includes the gentiles as G-d's Chosen People as follows:

> I tell you that the Kingdom of G-d will be taken away from you and given to the kind of people that will produce its fruit!
> -- Matthew 21:43-45 (CJB)

As time passed during his ministry and the Jewish nation began to reject Him as the prophesied 'King of the Jews,' Yeshua began concealing further truths from the Jewish people and to speak in parables.

Yeshua's solemn understanding of Isra'el's blindness and rejection by the Jewish leaders, the Pharisees and Sadducees, combined with G-d's plan of grace for the Gentiles was announced at Caesarea Philippi. A couple of months later during the last week before his crucifixion, he announced to the nation of Isra'el and its leaders:

> Yeshua said to them, "Haven't you ever read in the Tanakh, 'The very rock which the builders rejected has become the cornerstone! This has come from Adonai, and in our eyes it is amazing?' Therefore, I tell you that the Kingdom of G-d will be taken away from you and given to the kind of people that will

produce its fruit!"
-- Matthew 21:42-44 (CJB)

Yeshua wept over Jerusalem as he realized the awful fate that was to come to the nation of Isra'el because of their rejection of Mashiach. Once again, the conditional Covenant of the Land was to be enforced by G-d. But this time the Diaspora was to last two-thousand years—not a mere 70 years.

> Yerushalayim! Yerushalayim! You kill the prophets! You stone those who are sent to you! How often I wanted to gather your children, just as a hen gathers her chickens under her wings, but you refused!
> -- Matthew 23:37 (CJB)

Mashiach

Chapter 16
Messianic Judaism

Unfortunately, the priesthood in the first century C.E. had become completely unprincipled and unethical. Our ancestors focus was away from G-d and almost entirely on their desire to be free from the powerful Romans. They weren't looking for the spiritual relief that Mashiach had come to give.

Today, Christians have finally learned that Jews were not the "Christ-Killers" that brought on the Crusades or one of the embarrassing excuses that Hitler used to exterminate us in the Holocaust. To quote the *Algemeiner* website article dated June 13, 2013, entitled; "Christ Killers: the Hidden Agenda" as follows:

> The historic charge "Christ Killers" leveled against Jews is one of the most bizarre indictments ever made. Its defiance of facts

and logic would be comical if it weren't for the horrific slaughter of untold numbers of Jews over the centuries based on that accusation. Bizarre and illogical because statements and narratives in the New Testament itself contradict that claim. Trumping all accusations is the Christian doctrine that the crucifixion was dictated by prophesy—G-d commanded the crucifixion as part of His own divine plan.

Christians and Messianic Jews today have realized that ALL mankind was involved in what has been described as a conspiracy to put Yeshua to death even though He was completely innocent. In a new climate of reconciliation, both Christians and Jews need to understand how their distorted views have been conditioned by destructive forces that sought separation and opposition.

Even with this 'revelation' by Christians, they mostly still know little about the Jewish people during the Diaspora. However, many today are beginning to learn and understand what compelling reading the Jewish history is. Through the centuries, G-d has been clearly demonstrating His protective powers over the Jewish people, as well as their values and culture across every continent, and through all the incessant anti-Semitism. Indeed, it is certainly a miracle that our people have survived at all and are now returning to our homeland. These are clear signs of our confidence in Mashiach we have all expected and waited for.

On the other hand and to some extent, Christians

Mashiach

are ahead of us in our understanding, even of our own Abrahamic Covenant which was the promise of a special blessing for Abraham's descendants: a "chosen" people. Yet, they have seen G-d's blessing is obviously not for the Jewish peoples' benefit alone, but that, through us, all people would be blessed!

> Now Adonai said to Avram, Get yourself out of your country, away from your kinsmen and away from your father's house, and go to the land that I will show you. I will make of you a great nation, I will bless you, and I will make your name great; and you are to be a blessing. **I will bless those who bless you,** but I will curse anyone who curses you; and **by you all the families of the earth** will be blessed.
> -- Genesis 12:1-3 (CJB)

The promised benefit to the whole human race was later revealed as Mashiach—the "Suffering Servant" Yeshua willingly paid the penalty and made the ultimate sacrifice for our sins. That is, the promise to Abraham was really the promise of one unique seed, Mashiach, in whom all the covenants would find their fulfillment (Galatians 3:16). The theological term called the "eternal covenant" refers to an agreement within the G-dhead, made before the foundation of the world, out of which all the covenants with mankind would later flow. He made us, for His own. He draws us, to Himself, to enjoy and spend an eternity with Him in Heaven.

D.A. Osterman

Another question remains. If one has read the entire Torah and Tanakh with "Open Eyes" and still maintains an intentional disregard of the truths in the Torah and Tanakh, it is not only embarrassing but painful to ones soul to see its naivety, whether through blindness or intention. There is the question about Yeshua from today's rabbinical scholars: If Yeshua were indeed Mashiach, why is he not mentioned in any of our Jewish historical documents? This either reflects a degree of ignorance or an outright perversion of the truth. When a lowly lay person, like the author, can find these references, I am sure the learned Rabbis can find the same references and probably substantially more.

Rabbis of today point to the fact that no known manuscript of the Jerusalem Talmud makes mention of Yeshua, although one translation [Herford] has added it to Avodah Zarah 2:2 to align it with similar text of Chullin 2:22 in the Tosefta references to Yeshua in the uncensored texts of the Babylonian Talmud and the Tosefta.

But most know full well that in the Munich (1342 C.E.), Paris, and Jewish Theological Seminary of America manuscripts of the Talmud, the designation Ha-Notzri is added to the last mention of Yeshua in Sanhedrin 107b and Sotah 47a, as well as to the occurrences in Sanhedrin 43a, Sanhedrin 103a, Berachot 17b and Avodah Zarah 16b-17a.

While Notzri does not appear in the Tosefta by the time the Babylonian Talmud was produced, Notzri had become the standard Hebrew word for Christian, and Yeshua Ha-Notzri had become the conventional

Mashiach

rendition of "Yeshua the Nazarene" in Hebrew. For example, by 1180 C.E., the term Yeshua Ha-Notzri can be found in the Maimonides' Mishnah Torah (Hilchos Melachim 11:4, uncensored version).

The longstanding movement known as Messianic Judaism within the Jewish religion today is small in Isra'el. This sect reflects the belief that Yeshua is the promised Mashiach. Contrary to popular belief, Messianic Jews have not stopped being Jewish. In fact, they have kept a strong Jewish identity and lifestyle.

Fortunately for us 2,000 years ago, a tiny group of Isra'eli disciples of Yeshua obeyed what the L-rd had commanded, to spread the good news - "the gospel" from Isra'el to the rest of the world. Their obedience changed the world forever. And now in the last days as prophesied, the L-rd is pouring out His Spirit upon the descendants of Abraham, Isaac, and Jacob; and Isra'eli disciples of Yeshua are once again heeding the call and command to spread the good news and the foundation of their faith to the people of Isra'el, and to the world.

Unfortunately for us Jews, the Messianic movement within our Jewish religion during the first century was turned upside-down, and the voice of Jewish believers was all but silenced, leading to a great disconnect with the rest of the Christian world. Today the primary work being done in Isra'el to deliver the information about Yeshua as Mashiach, however, is not through Christian missions. It is being done through local Jewish Messianic congregations. The larger ones are in Tiberias, K'far Saba, Netanya, Jerusalem and Jaffa. *Charisma News* reports there are 150-plus congregations in Isra'el, of whom about 60 percent speak Russian as their first language. I have included a partial list of 50+ of Messianic congregations (see Appendix B) around Isra'el meeting in different languages. The number of believers varies. Moishe Rosen, founder of a San Francisco-based organization that recognizes Yeshua as Mashiach, has estimated there are about 60,000 Jewish believers in Yeshua worldwide. Others have estimated that there are around 20,000 within Isra'el and a total of close to 500,000 globally. As you can see with this wide variation, no one knows for certain; but everyone agrees the numbers are growing exponentially. Within Isra'el a fairly good estimate shows that it grew from 1948 when there were only 12 Jews who believed in Yeshua which could be counted, increasing through to the year 1987 C.E. when there were an estimated 3,000 and continued to grow further to 5000 Messianic Jews by 1997 C.E., increasing to today's approximate 20,000 Yeshua adherents.

Many Jews ask, what is the difference between Messianic Judaism and Gentile Christianity? In the simplest explanation, gentile Christianity is the faith in Yeshua as expressed by gentile followers of Him. Gentile Christianity today numbers over one billion people in the world, with innumerable denominations and doctrines, all centered on Yeshua as Savior. For most of the first century C.E., faith in Yeshua was predominantly Jewish. As more and more gentiles came into the Messianic faith, most had no understanding of its Jewish roots or how it was through G-d's eternal covenant with the people of Isra'el that they were being blessed.

Messianic Judaism is really not Christianity in the ecclesiastical sense. Messianic Judaism doesn't follow the Christian church customs or use the Christian religious calendar. For example, Messianic Judaism does not celebrate Christmas or Easter. Rather, it celebrates Jewish holidays, and observes Shabbat and the dietary laws as our people have done since Sinai. Although we have our own understanding of the Torah and Tanakh, Messianic Judaism is no different from other branches of Judaism that put their own modern interpretations to the Jewish bible.

Over time, the gentile separation from our Jewish roots eventually led to the formation of a second wing of our faith - what we know today as Christianity. Messianic Jews have maintained a more traditional Jewish expression of faith in Yeshua as Mashiach. Messianic Judaism holds that it is VERY Jewish to believe in Yeshua. Messianic Jews observe the feasts and holidays of the Tanakh while at the same time maintaining that the only true Mashiach is Yeshua.

Messianic Judaism affirms that the Jewish people have been, are, and will always be the chosen people of G-d. The only nation G-d ever linked His name to in the Torah and Tanakh is Isra'el, where he called Himself, the G-d of Isra'el. The scriptures tell us His promises to Isra'el are eternal and extend to the sons of Jacob, the House of Isra'el, known today as the Jewish People.

In addition to those that profess to be associated with one of the estimated 150 congregations of

Messianic Jews within Isra'el, there are a great many Isra'eli Jews who silently believe that Yeshua was indeed Mashiach. No one knows how many for sure, for like the Pharisee Nicodemus in the first century, they are keeping their beliefs to themselves, for the time being. This will continue to be true, as additional prophecy must be fulfilled, and there must be 12,000 from each of the tribes of Isra'el brought to believe Yeshua is Mashiach, and converted, before Mashiach appears again. This includes the 12,000 people from the tribe of JUDAH, and 12,000 from the tribe of LEVI. This will be a difficult task to accomplish. While most of the tribes of JUDAH and LEVI today are Jewish, all the other tribes are from the "lost ten tribes" which migrated into Europe, Russia, Great Britain, Australia and America! Promised in Revelation 7:1-9 (CJB):

> After this, I saw four angels standing at the four corners of the earth, holding back the four winds of the earth, so that no wind would blow on the land, on the sea or on any tree. I saw another angel coming up from the east with a seal from the living G-d, and he shouted to the four angels who had been given power to harm the land and the sea, "Do not harm the land or the sea or the trees until we have sealed the servants of our G-d on their foreheads!" I heard how many were sealed — 144,000 from every tribe of the people of Isra'el:
>
> | | |
> |---|---|
> | From the tribe of Y'hudah | 12,000 |
> | from the tribe of Re'uven | 12,000 |

from the tribe of Gad,	12,000
from the tribe of Asher	12,000
from the tribe of Naftali	12,000
from the tribe of M'nasheh	12,000
from the tribe of Shim'on	12,000
from the tribe of Levi	12,000
from the tribe of Yissakhar	12,000
from the tribe of Z'vulun	12,000
from the tribe of Yosef	12,000
from the tribe of Binyamin	12,000

After this, I looked; and there before me was a huge crowd, too large for anyone to count, from every nation, tribe, people and language. They were standing in front of the throne and in front of the Lamb, dressed in white robes and holding palm branches in their hands."

May G-d speed this day of reconciliation and unity!

Messianic Jews believe that Yeshua will return as King sitting on His throne in Isra'el when this reconciliation occurs. When Yeshua was put on trial before the high court of the Jews, and the high priest demanded to know whether Yeshua was the Christ, the Son of G-d,

Yeshua said to him, 'The words are your own. But I tell you that one day you will see the Son of Man sitting at the right hand of HaG'vurah and coming on the clouds of heaven.'
-- Matthew 26:64 (CJB)

D.A. Osterman

Yeshua knew that the Jewish religious leaders would understand this to be a reference to the book of Daniel, where the Daniel prophet wrote:

> I saw in the night visions, and behold, there came with the clouds of the sky one like a son of man, and he came even to the ancient of days, and they brought him near before him. There was given him dominion, and glory, and a kingdom that all the peoples, nations, and languages should serve him: his dominion is an everlasting dominion, which shall not pass away, and his kingdom that which shall not be destroyed.   -- Daniel 7:13-14 (CJB)

While Yeshua is denied by most Jews, many of Judaism's top philosophers and teachers have had deep appreciation of him. Here are just two of them, starting with the highly respected Jewish philosopher Martin Buber who wrote:

> From my youth onwards I have found in Yeshua my great brother. That Christianity has regarded and does regard him as G-d and Moshi'a has always appeared to me a fact of the highest importance which, for his sake and my own, I must endeavor to understand...I am more than ever certain that a great place belongs to him in Isra'el's history of faith and that this place cannot be described by any of the usual categories.

Mashiach

The former president of Hebrew Union College, Rabbi Kaufman Kohler addressed the U.S. Congress in 1893 in the following fashion:

> No ethical system or religious catechism, however broad and pure, could equal the efficiency of this great personality, standing, unlike any other, midway between heaven and earth, equally near to G-d and to man...Jesus, the helper of the poor, the friend of the sinner, the brother of every fellow-sufferer, the comforter of every sorrow-laden, the healer of the sick, the up-lifter of the fallen, the lover of man, the redeemer of woman, won the heart of mankind by storm. Jesus, the meekest of men, the most despised of the despised race of the Jews, mounted the world's throne to be earth's Great King.

The next great step—and simple conclusion—would be to accept Yeshua as Mashiach.

In the first century one of the key debates was whether a Gentile had to become a Jew to embrace Yeshua as Mashiach. Today, the question is whether a Jew must become a Gentile to be a follower of Yeshua. During just the last 20 years, as significant change has taken place within Messianic Jewish congregations and among Jewish believers in Yeshua, there is no longer a desire to just become assimilated members of Christian churches. Indeed, Jewish believers in Yeshua want to be Jewish through and through. The Lausanne Movement stressed the validity of culture and cultural identification. And that was the start of the Messianic Jewish congregations.

In closing, Meno Kalisher, one of the Messianic rabbis in Jerusalem stated:

> The situation in Jerusalem will decide … the situation in the rest of the world. The reason the Tanakh says pray for the peace of Jerusalem (Psalm 122:7) is because it's like praying 'Mashiach come soon.' And when He comes soon there will be peace in Jerusalem. There will be peace in the rest of the world.

The Talmud states that on our individual "Judgment Day," after the soul departs from the body, one of the questions G-d will ask us is: Did you anticipate the redemption?" [Babylonian Talmud - Tractate Shabbos 31a]. Why, however, should this question be asked of us? Is it a mitzvah—Divine mandate—to believe in the coming of Mashiach and the future redemption? An answer can be found in the first of the "Ten Mandates" which were spoken at Mount Sinai as follows:

> I am Adonai your G-d, who brought you out of the land of Egypt, out of the abode of slavery.
> -- Exodus 20:2 (CJB)

Over 50 prayers a day are said in reference to the coming of Mashiach. We pray for our redemption as

Mashiach

the 12th principle of our Yigdal prayers: "I believe with complete faith in the coming of Mashiach. And though he may tarry, I shall wait anticipating his arrival each day," may Adonai make us worthy of reaching the days of Mashiach and deliver our redemption today.

ANI MA'AMIN

I believe with complete faith
In the coming of the Messiah, I believe
Believe in the coming of the Messiah
In the coming of the Messiah, I believe
Believe in the coming of the Messiah
And even though he may tarry
Nonetheless I will wait for him
And even though he may tarry
Nonetheless I will wait for him
Nonetheless, I will wait for him
I will wait every day for him to come
Nonetheless, I will wait for him
I will wait every day for him to come
I believe (Ani Ma'amin)

Look! I am sending my messenger to clear the way before me; and the L-rd, whom you seek, will suddenly come to his temple. Yes, the messenger of the covenant, in whom you take such delight — look! Here he comes, says Adonai-Tzva'ot.   -- Malachi 3:1 (CJB)

In the last few centuries, it is the rare Jewish person

who would consider the Messianic Jewish message of Yeshua's teachings. However, today, new generations of Jewish people are living in the free world and being less persecuted than their parents and grandparents. We are more informed and open minded.

If you have read to this point in the book, you most likely are a nonjudgmental Jew who is interested in looking for answers. Yet you may still feel it's wrong to go against the thinking of Jewish authorities you trust. Or you might be saying, "It's just not Jewish to believe Yeshua is Mashiach;" or you might even have said, "I'm just not interested in knowing about Yeshua."

In truth, as an open-minded articulate person, you're determined to expand your mind and explore possibilities. Life is comprised of many things, and you have thoughts, ideas, and beliefs about them. But have you really examined them? Have you found the answers you have been looking for? I invite you to read the complete story of Yeshua for yourself as it is presented in the first four books of the Brit Chadasha. Pray to G-d, telling Him of your doubts and questions about Yeshua, and sincerely asking Him the question, **Is Yeshua truly Ben Elohim?** G-d will show you the truth as you read. As King David prayed in the book of Psalms 25:4-5:

> Make me know your ways, Adonai, teach me your paths. Guide me in your truth, and teach me; for you are the G-d who saves me, my hope is in you all day long.
>
> -- Psalms 25:4-5 (CJB)

Mashiach

Why is Yeshua so important? He wasn't just another Rabbi, philosopher, prophet, or just a truly good man. Messianic Jews today believe **Yeshua died willingly as a sacrifice for our sins**, for it is our sins that separate us from G-d "The Holy One" (הקדוש). We need to understand that G-d is infinitely holy and we are unholy. There is no way an unholy person may come into the presence of our infinitely holy G-d without forgiveness: "Your eyes are too pure to see evil, you cannot countenance oppression." (Habakkuk 1:13 CJB).

So how can we possibly approach an all holy G-d? Only through G-d's way, which is not through our own personal zeal, emotions, attending synagogue regularly, faithfully following the Halachah praying three times every day, or working to do positive things in life. It is only through the blood sacrifice G-d made for *all* of us by sending Ben Elohim to die as the "Suffering Servant" on the cross. Without the grace of G-d and His sacrifice of Ben Elohim, no one can come into the presence of HaKadosh, and we will be eternally separated from "The Holy One." Just because we are already "G-d's chosen people" as a nation, doesn't mean any particular individual Jewish person is to be saved.

So what is our standing as Jews with G-d? We still firmly remain G-d's chosen people, and we have a priority over Gentiles in that Mashiach himself, Yeshua, came first as a Jew to the Jews. In the Brit Chadasha book of Romans 9:4-5 (CJB), the author Paul (formerly the Jewish Pharisee Saul) brings a list of privileges to a climax with these words:

> ...the people of Isra'el! They were made G-d's
> children, the Sh'khinah has been with them,
> the covenants are theirs, likewise the giving of
> the Torah, the Temple service and the
> promises; the Patriarchs are theirs; and from
> them, as far as his physical descent is
> concerned, came the Messiah, who is over all.
> Praised be Adonai forever! Amen.

The Mashiach Yeshua was a Jew, and a Son of
David. He focused his earthly ministry on the Jews.
Isra'elites had a priority in his work. In Matthew 10:5-
6, Yeshua says to the twelve apostles as he sends them
out on a mission, "Do not go in the way of the Gentiles,
and do not enter any city of the Samaritans; but rather
go to the lost sheep of the house of Isra'el." And in
Matthew 15:24, Yeshua says, "I was sent only to the
lost sheep of the house of Isra'el." So during his
earthly life, Yeshua was focused *on* the Jews. *They* had
priority in his ministry.

However, salvation for **all** humanity is *from* the
Jews. In the Brit Chadasha book of Romans 11:17-24,
Paul compares the Jewish nation to an olive tree. He
says that natural branches are broken off and unnatural
branches were grafted in, meaning that Jews by birth
were unbelieving and so cut off from the covenant of
promise; and the Gentiles who believed were grafted in
and saved by the covenant of promise. Verses 17-18
are crucial for Gentiles as follows:

Mashiach

> If some of the branches were broken off, and
> [a Gentile], being a wild olive, were grafted in
> among them and became partaker with them of
> the rich root of the olive tree, [then Gentiles]
> do not be arrogant toward the branches; but if
> you are arrogant, remember that it is not you
> who supports the root, but the root supports
> you.

In other words, salvation comes to the Gentiles from the
root of G-d's covenant with the Jews. Gentiles are
simply grafted in like wild olive branches that have no
historical claim at all to being G-d's people. Yet G-d
saved Gentiles by reckoning them as children of
Abraham simply by faith, as Paul says in Galatians 3:7,
"It is those who are of faith who are sons of Abraham."
So while Jews have priority, we Jews we have a heavy
responsibility that G-d gave us to save the people of the
world through our covenant with Abraham.

The Mashiach, Our Deliverer, our Moshi'a Yeshua,
came to the world as a Jew for Jews. Mashiach
Yeshua, however, brought salvation to all mankind
through us as Jews. This awesome responsibility
carries an equally awesome consequence or warning:
The Jews will enter first into final judgment and final
blessing. We must fear G-d. When we disrespect G-d
or fail to fear His authority as Supreme in the universe,
we reduce him to the world's standard of a god...and
that could be anything you hold onto as idols.

As I personally walk with the L-rd, I have
discovered G-d's ominous threat is not to me as his

creation, but to my ego and my sinful nature. His infinite authority and power are displayed to rescue me from my delusions of self-righteousness and to reveal the truth that "un-blinds" me and sets me free.

In the end, G-d will Judge. Furthermore, while He is a righteous Judge, because of His holiness, He cannot compromise with our sins. Every sin that we have committed since birth will be brought into justice. Fortunately, in 21st century parlance, we have an advocate, a lawyer, who will represent us on judgement day, Yeshua. Through a belief in Yeshua, our sins can be forgiven and cleansed. Indeed, our slate of sins will be wiped clean as if they never happened. "**I will be merciful toward their wickednesses and remember their sins no more**" (Hebrews 8:12 and Jeremiah 31:30-34). Belief in Him wipes out all sins! We are left with a clean soul, and His illuminating Holy Spirit.

And because of Yeshua's resurrection, death's power over us will be eliminated. Yeshua himself tells us in Mark 12:25 that people will rise from the dead and be like angels in heaven. We will never die, but have eternal life the moment we accept the fact that Yeshua is Mashiach.

What a wonderful splendid future! How simple a decision to make in order to claim your eternal future with Yeshua in heaven. "Eternal life is this: to know you, the one true G-d, and him whom you sent, Yeshua the Messiah" (John 17:3). Eternal life! Yeshua's words ring out to everyone right now: "This is the will of my Father: that all who see the Son and trust in him should have eternal life, and that I should raise them up on the Last Day" (John 6:40). What does a person need to do? One decision—a simple mental choice: Trust in Yeshua as Mashiach.

If you are looking for peace, this is a way to balance your life. No one can be perfect or have a perfect life. Fortunately, Elohim has put within us a deep desire to know Him. If you would like to explore Yeshua by opening your mind even further to His transforming power. When you do, you will discover Yeshua's words are true: "I AM the Way— and the Truth and the Life; no one comes to the Father except through me" (John 14:6 CJB).

If you the reader are in Isra'el and this dialog is of interest to you, several Messianic Congregations can be found in every major Isra'eli population center, from Jezreal in the north to Eilat in the south and all the major cities in between, with multiple congregations in Tel Aviv, Jaffa, Jerusalem and Haifa.

There is a list of approximately 50 congregations shown in Appendix B. If you're reading this in North America, almost every city has several Messianic Jewish Synagogues. Most who look into these and visit, immediately learn they don't have to give up their G-d-given Jewish identity by following Yeshua, and find they will actually enhance it by becoming the kind of Jewish person that the G-d of Isra'el, the G-d of Abraham, Isaac, and wants.

So if you have been longing for the coming of Mashiach, then pray for the veil to be lifted from your eyes and the eyes of all the Jewish people and for the peace of Jerusalem;

On that day his feet will stand on the Mount of Olives, which lies to the east of Yerushalayim…
Then Adonai will be king over the whole world. On that day Adonai will be the only one, and his name will be the only name.
-- Zechariah 14:4 & 9 (CJB)

Yeshua, the Jewish Moshi'a has extended His grace to all mankind, and He will return on the day mankind calls out:

Baruch Haba B'Shem Adonai
(Blessed is He who comes in the Name of the L-rd)

SHALOM

Mashiach

About the Author

D. A. Osterman (אוסטרמן ד) lived the first 11 years of his life in Minnesota, U.S.A. Both his grandfathers relocated to the U.S. from Sweden in the early 1900s.

His earliest ancestors in the "old country" were eastern Ashkenazic Jews. The Osterman name is the Jewish variant of *Oster* or *Ost* which adds the Yiddish "man" to the end of the name. The origins come from a nickname from Polish, *Ostry*, meaning *brilliant* or *sharp-minded*.

D. A. Osterman's grandfather on his mother's side was a theologian and scholar, and on his father's side an industrious railroad worker. His parents passed down an admiration and respect for the Bible. Instilling values and a work ethic in him at an early age, and teaching him, "Don't take things at face value" along with a deep reverence for G-d."

In the 1950s, he and his family moved to Santa Barbara, California. The rest of his school years were spent doing research and studying physics in college. In 1978, he received his M.B.A. from Pepperdine University. Osterman's biblical upbringing, his early lessons not to take things at face value, and his background in research, comes through and is reflected in his debut inspirational book, *Mashiach*.

"One man's candle is light for many."
– Talmud on Shabbat

D.A. Osterman

Appendix A
44 Prophecies of Mashiach
From the Torah & Tanakh

The following table lists 44 of the hundreds of prophecies of Mashiach Yeshua contained in the Torah and Tanakh and later confirmed in the Brit Chadasha.

44 Prophecies of Mashiach Yeshua Fulfilled		
Prophecies About Yeshua	Torah/Tanakh Scripture	Brit Chadasha Fulfillment
1 Mashiach would be born of a woman.	Genesis 3:15	Matthew 1:20 Galatians 4:4
2 Mashiach would be born in Bethlehem.	Micah 5:2	Matthew 2:1 Luke 2:4-6
3 Mashiach would be born of a virgin.	Isaiah 7:14	Matthew 1:22-23 Luke 1:26-31
4 Mashiach would come from the line of Abraham.	Genesis 12:3 Genesis 22:18	Matthew 1:1 Romans 9:5
5 Mashiach would be a descendant of Isaac.	Genesis 17:19 Genesis 21:12	Luke 3:34
6 Mashiach would be a	Numbers 24:17	Matthew 1:2

Mashiach

	descendant of Jacob.		
7	Mashiach would come from the tribe of Judah.	Genesis 49:10	Luke 3:33 Hebrews 7:14
8	Mashiach would be heir to King David's throne.	2 Samuel 7:12-13 Isaiah 9:7	Luke 1:32-33 Romans 1:3
9	Messiah's throne will be anointed and eternal.	Psalm 45:6-7 Daniel 2:44	Luke 1:33 Hebrews 1:8-12
10	Mashiach would be called Immanuel.	Isaiah 7:14	Matthew 1:23
11	Mashiach would spend a season in Egypt.	Hosea 11.1	Matthew 2:14-15
12	A massacre of children would happen at Mashiach's birthplace.	Jeremiah 31:15	Matthew 2:16-18
13	A messenger would prepare the way for Mashiach	Isaiah 40:3-5	Luke 3:3-6
14	Mashiach would be rejected by his own people.	Psalm 69:8 Isaiah 53:3	John 1:11 John 7:5
15	Mashiach would be a prophet.	Deuteronomy 18:15	Acts 3:20-22
16	Mashiach would be preceded	Malachi 4:5-6	Matthew

	by Elijah.		11:13-14
17	Mashiach would be declared the Son of G-d.	Psalm 2:7	Matthew 3:16-17
18	Mashiach would be called a Nazarene.	Isaiah 11:1	Matthew 2:23
19	Mashiach would bring light to Galilee.	Isaiah 9:1-2	Matthew 4:13-16
20	Mashiach would speak in parables.	Psalm 78:2-4 Isaiah 6:9-10	Matthew 13:10-15, 34-35
21	Mashiach would be sent to heal the brokenhearted.	Isaiah 61:1-2	Luke 4:18-19
22	Mashiach would be a priest after the order of Melchizedek.	Psalm 110:4	Hebrews 5:5-6
23	Mashiach would be called King.	Psalm 2:6 Zechariah 9:9	Matthew 27:37 Mark 11:7-11
24	Mashiach would be praised by little children.	Psalm 8:2	Matthew 21:16
25	Mashiach would be betrayed.	Psalm 41:9 Zechariah 11:12-13	Luke 22:47-48 Matthew 26:14-16
26	Messiah's price money would	Zechariah	Matthew 27:9-

Mashiach

	be used to buy a potter's field.	11:12-13	10
27	Mashiach would be falsely accused.	Psalm 35:11	Mark 14:57-58
28	Mashiach would be silent before his accusers.	Isaiah 53:7	Mark 15:4-5
29	Mashiach would be spat upon and struck.	Isaiah 50:6	Matthew 26:67
30	Mashiach would be hated without cause.	Psalm 35:19 Psalm 69:4	John 15:24-25
31	Mashiach would be crucified with criminals.	Isaiah 53:12	Matthew 27:38 Mark 15:27-28
32	Mashiach would be given vinegar to drink.	Psalm 69:21	Matthew 27:34 John 19:28-30
33	Mashiach's hands and feet would be pierced.	Psalm 22:16 Zechariah 12:10	John 20:25-27
34	Mashiach would be mocked and ridiculed.	Psalm 22:7-8	Luke 23:35
35	Soldiers would gamble for Messiah's garments.	Psalm 22:18	Luke 23:34 Matthew 27:35-36
36	Mashiach's bones would not	Exodus 12:46	John 19:33-36

	be broken.	Psalm 34:20	
37	Mashiach would be forsaken by G-d.	Psalm 22:1	Matthew 27:46
38	Mashiach would pray for his enemies.	Psalm 109:4	Luke 23:34
39	Soldiers would pierce Mashiach's side.	Zechariah 12:10	John 19:34
40	Mashiach would be buried with the rich.	Isaiah 53:9	Matthew 27:57-60
41	Mashiach would resurrect from the dead.	Psalm 16:10 Psalm 49:15	Matthew 28:2-7 Acts 2:22-32
42	Mashiach would ascend to heaven.	Psalm 24:7-10	Mark 16:19 Luke 24:51
43	Mashiach would be seated at G-d's right hand.	Psalm 68:18 Psalm 110:1	Mark 16:19 Matthew 22:44
44	Mashiach would be a sacrifice for sin.	Isaiah 53:5-12	Romans 5:6-8

Appendix B
Messianic Jewish Congregations
Listed Alphabetically by City

This is a list of Orthodox Jewish congregations that are Believers in Mashiach Yeshua in Isra'el which the author currently knows of. This is by no means a comprehensive list, and apologies to those who were left out. If you are not listed and would like to be shown in future printings of the book, there will be at least 1 or 2 changes and new printings each year. Please send an email to the publishers representative about your congregation that you would like to have listed, corrected or changed at: davidcohen7831@gmail.com

There are also many home groups and small organizations which do not necessarily advertise themselves (some are not listed for security reasons); however, by building relationships with established groups you will learn more about them.

Disclaimer:

Just like everywhere else, not all congregations and leaders agree on everything. The Author believes that those listed here all believe in the essentials of the Messianic Jewish faith and the need to share the gospel with Isra'elis (Jews and Arabs) and the Nations. The Author has not screened these entries; therefore the author cannot endorse any of these groups. The purpose of this list is to allow the reader to simply use it as a starting point and go where the L-rd leads.

Ariel

Kehilat Ariel
Rechov Avner 1/25
Ariel
Isra'el
Phone: 03-9364771
Shabbat 6:30pm &
Wednesday Bible Study
7:30pm
Hebrew with English,
Arabic
& Russian translation

Ashdod

Derech v'Emet (Russian)
(The Way and Truth)
Leaders: Oleg & Olga Hazin
Website:
http://wayandtruth.org/
Contact thru website or
Messianic Jewish Movement
Int'l
800-4 –YESHUA

Beit Hallel
Congregation
(House of Praise)

Leader: Isra'el Pochtar
P.O. Box 14179, Ashdod
77700 Isra'el
Phone #: 972 526 243 602
email:
voj.admin@gmail.com
Website: http://vojisrael.com

Beer Sheva (Negev)

Beer Sheva
Messianic
Congregation (Negev)

Leaders Howard and Randi
Bass
P.O. Box 810
Beer Sheva
84607
Isra'el
Phone: 07-627-7022
songfish@netvision.net.il
Hebrew with Russian,
Romanian
and English translation

Carmiel

Nachalei Mayim
Chayim

Call for directions
Carmiel
Isra'el
Phone: 04-9586242
rolw@barak-online.net
Shabbat service 10am &
Tuesday 7pm
Russian with Hebrew and
English translation

Mashiach

B'nei Torah
Ishmael Mizrahi
Netiv HaLotus 17/4
Carmiel Isra'el
phone: + 972 4 958 6165
bnei_torah@hotmail.com

Kehilat HaDerech
POB 502,
Carmiel
20101
Isra'el
Fax: 04-988-8980
Shabbat 10:30am
Hebrew with translation
to Hungarian,
English, Spanish,
Russian & Romanian

Kehilat HaDerech (Congregation of the Way)
Leader: Yossi Ovadia
Address: P.O. Box 502
Karmiel 20101
Phone #: 972-4-988-5916
Email:
Office@kehilatHaderech.org
Website:
www.kehilathaderech.org

Naharei Maim Haim, Isra'el (Rivers of Living Water, Isra'el)
Leaders: Irene Friedman
Phone #: 972-4-998-1374
Email: rolw@012.net.il

Eilat

Kehilat Eilat & The Shelter (Hostel) (Congregation of Eilat)
Leaders: John and Judi Pex
Address: P.O. Box 816 in
Eilat 88104
Phone #: 972-8-637-2859
Email:
info@shelterhostel.com
Website:
www.shelterhostel.com

Way Truth and Life (Messianic Russian Olim congregation)
Leaders: Yuri and Marina
Volodarsky
Email: wtl@012.net.il
Phone #: 972-50-455-0842

Haifa

Beit Eliyahu, Haifa
Elder: Shlomo Drori,
PO Box 525,
31004
Haifa,
Isra'el
Phone +972-4-52-35-81
Hebrew with Russian,
Romanian & English
translation

New Life Fellowship
P.O. Box 4270
Haifa
31042
+970-4-838-7850
vredko@aol.com
Russian with English &
Hebrew translation

Beit Eliahu
(House of Elijah)
Leader: Shmuel Aweida
Address: Mayer 41 Haifa
German Colony 33333
Phone #: 972-54-470-6917
website:
http://www.beiteliahu.org

Kehilat HaCarmel
(Congregation of the
Carmel)
Leaders: David Davis

and Peter Tsukahira
Address: P.O. Box 7004
Haifa, 31070
Email:
kcarmel@netvision.net.il
Website:
www.carmel-assembly.org.il

Nazarene Church (Arabic)
Leader: Botrus Ghrieb
Address: 16 Hagenim Street
Haifa
Phone #: 972-4-853-3931

New Covenant Church (Arabic)
Leader: Yousef Dakwar
Address: P.O. Box 99730
Haifa 31996
Email:
contact@haifancc.org
Website: www.haifancc.org

Jaffa

Shavei Tzion
(Return to Zion)
Leader: Leon Mazin
Phone #: 972-50-201-0261
Email:
tsionsh@netvision.net.il
Website:
www.shaveitzion.org
Jaffa

Mashiach

Beit Immanuel Congregation

Leader David Lazarus.
8 Auerbach Street
POB 2773
Jaffo
61027
Isra'el
Phone: 03-672-7183
Fax: 03-672-7183
Email:
welcome@beitimmanuel.org
Website:
www.beitimmanuel.org
Erev Shabbat 7pm, Sun.
prayer 7pm
Hebrew with English &
Russian translations

Jaffa Assembly

P.O. Box 8185
Jaffa, 61081,
Isra'el.
Phone: 972-3-6827146
(in Isra'el: 03 6827146)
Email: kmyt@walla.co.il

Jerusalem

Ahavat Yeshua (Love of Jesus)

Leader: Asher Intrater
Email:
revive.israel@revive-
israel.org
Website: www.revive-

israel.org
Jerusalem

Beit Geulah (House of Redemption)

Leader: Meno Kalisher
Email: meno@actcom.co.il
Phone: 972-2-583-4949
POB 31878, Jerusalem,
91317
Jerusalem
Hebrew with Russian &
English translation

Beit HaYeshua (House of Salvation)

Leader: Zvi Randelman
Address: P.O. Box 25,
Maale Adumim, 98100
Phone #: 972-2-678-1046
Email: zvir@013.net.il
Website:
www.beit-hayeshua.org

Calvary Chapel Jerusalem

Pastor Brad Antolovitch
POB 1429
Jerusalem,
Isra'el 91013
Phone/Fax: 972-2-679-4718
Email:
forzion@netvision.net.il
Tuesdays & Shabbat at 6pm

219

Christ Church
Leader: David Pileggi
Address: P.O. Box 14037
Jerusalem 94140
Phone #: 972-0-2-626-1959
Email:
churchsecretary@cmj-israel.org

Jerusalem Messianic Assembly
Senior Elder: Victor Smadja
56 Prophets Street,
Jerusalem,
Isra'el
Hebrew with English translation

Kehilat El Roii (Congregation of The G-d who Sees)
Leader: Ofer Amitai
Phone: 972 (2) 678-7229
Email:
congregation.elroii@gmail.com

Kehilat Even Yisrael (Congregation of the Rock of Isra'el)
Leader: Victor Blum
Baptist House Center,
Narkis St 4
Jerusalem
Isra'el
Phone #: 972 (2) 651-1536

Email:
victo_nm@netvision.net.il
website:
www.gratefullygrafted.org
Erev Shabat Friday 6:30pm,
prayer Mon. 6:30pm
Russian speaking congregation
(translations into English/ Hebrew/ Finnish/ German)

Kehilat ha'Seh al Har Zion (Congregation of the Lamb on Mount Zion)
Leaders: Benjamin/Reuven Berger
Address: P.O. Box 9542
Jerusalem 91094
Phone #: 972-2-627-7747
Email:
betavara@netvision.net.il

Kehilat Kol BaMidbar (Voice in the Wilderness)
Leader: Anthony Simon
P.O. Box 31699, Jerusalem, 91316
Phone #: 972-5-428-2803
Email:
nahum2@hotmail.com
Website:
www.voice-wilderness.com
sermon in English translated to Russian

Mashiach

Kehilat Shalhevetyah
P.O. Box 584,
Jerusalem,
91004.
972-2-6792935.
Hebrew with Finnish &
English translation

King of Kings
Leader: Wayne Hilsden
Address: P.O. Box 427
Jerusalem, 91003
Phone #: 972-2-625-1899
Email: kkcj@kkcj.org
Website: www.kkcj.org

Narkis Street Congregation
Leader: Chuck Kopp
4 Narkis Street (Baptist
House Center)
P.O. Box 1118
Jerusalem
Isra'el
Phone: +972- 2-231-680
Shabbat 10:30am
Hebrew with English
translation through headset
Email: mail@narkis.org
Website: www.narkis.org

Neve Tzion Congregation
P.O. Box 31489,
Jerusalem, 91314 ISRA'EL
Tele: 011-972-2-679-6319
Leader: Ariel

ffoz@netvision.net.il
English with Hebrew prayers

Shekinah Fellowship
Mike Lambert
P.O. Box 4416
Jerusalem
91040
02-345619
Roeh Yisrael
(Shepherd of Isra'el)
Leader: Joe Shulam
Address: P.O. Box 8043
Jerusalem 91080
Phone #: 972-2-623-1019
FAX: 972-2-6249258
Email:
shulam@actcom.co.il
Website: www.netivyah.org
Service in Hebrew with
English

Jezreal Valley
(Valley of Armageddon)

Shaar HaEmek Congregation
Leader: Isra'el Harel
Email: iharel7@gmail.com
Website :
www.harelfamily.net

K'far Saba

Tikvat Shomron Ariel
Pastor: Henry
054-632698
Meetings: Friday, 19:00
Kehilat Ha Ma'ayan
Elders Tony Sperandeo
Call for directions
Kfar Saba
Isra'el
Phone: 09-7662351
Fax: +972-9-7662350
Email:
hamaayan@netvision.net.il
Website: www.kehilat-
hamaayan.org.il
Shabbat 11am
Hebrew with Russian &
English translation

Keren Yeshua, Kfar Saba
Noam Hendren,
P.O. Box 637,
Kfar Saba,
Isra'el
Service in Hebrew only

Kiriat Gat

Rehovot Messianic Fellowship
Meeting in Rehovot on

Saturday evenings at 1800
Phone: 058-260369
jake_israel@yahoo.com
Kehilat Kol BaMidbar,
Kiriat Gat
Call for directions
Kiriat Gat, Isra'el
antony@internet-zahav.net
Phone: 02-6222367
English and Russian

Kiryat Yam

Ohalei Rachamim
Call for directions
Kiryat Yam
Isra'el
Phone: 04-8777921
Hebrew with Russian
translation

Natzeret Illit

Ruach Hachaim (Spirit of Life)
Leader: Sergei Bosharniko
Phone #: 972-4-645-0471
Email:
bargbros@netvision.net.il
Rechov Agmon, 20 aleph,
Apt.4
Natzeret Illit
17801 Isra'el
Phone: 06-6450471
Russian & Hebrew worship

Mashiach

Kehilah Meshichit Ahava

Hazabar St. 10/1 (entrance on the Gesher nof Yisrael).
PO Box 603
Natzeret Illit
Isra'el
Phone: +972-6-655-28-52
mjcahava@internetzahav.il
Shabbat 10am
Hebrew, Russian and English

Netanya

Beit Asaf

Leaders Evan Thomas, David Loden, Paul Liberman
POB 13908, Netanya, Isra'el
Phone #: 972-9-885-0029
Fax: +972-9-8616420
Email:
emthom@netvision.net.il
Website:
www.beit-asaph.org.il
Services: Shabbat 10:30am, Hebrew with English & Russian translations

Poriya

Kehilat Poriya (Congregation of Poriya)

Leaders: Eric and Terri Morey
Email:
info@TheGalileeExperience.com
Contact: Tents of Mercy
Website:
www.tents-of-mercy.org

Rishon L'Tzion

Grace and Truth Christian Congregation

Leader: Baruch Maoz
Phone #: 972-3-966-1898
Email:
gracetr@attglobal.net
Meeting Place: Rechov Shkolnick 8, Rishon L'Tzion Isra'el
Phone: 03-9661898 Fax: 03-9661898
bmaoz@attglobal.net
Shabbat Service 10:30am
Hebrew with translation to Russian & English

Tel Aviv

Adonai Roi (The Lord is My Shepherd)

Leader: Avi Mizrachi
Phone #: 972-3-621-2100
Email: dugit@zahav.net.il
Website: www.dugit.org

Brit Olam Fellowship (Eternal Covenant Fellowship)

Leader: Jacques Elbaz
The City Hotel(downtown),
9 Mapu St.
P.O. Box 5023,
Tel Aviv
61050
Isra'el
Phone: 972-3-524-5283
Shabbat 10am Hebrew with English translation

Ethiopian Jewish Messianic Congregation

Meherati Radi
Call for directions
Tel Aviv
Isra'el
Phone: 052-946598
Service in Amharic

Kehilat Adonai Roi

Leader Avi Mizrachi
Dugit: Frishman St. 43,
POB 11174
Tel Aviv, Isra'el
Phone: 03-523-7586
Fax: 03-522-8738
Shabbat 5pm
Hebrew with English translation

Kehilat Har Tsion, Tel Aviv

Leaders: Baruch and Dominique Bierman.
Meeting at 15 Sintat Alley,
Har Tsion,
Tel Aviv, Isra'el
Erev Shabbat 7pm,
Shabbat 6pm, Sunday 8pm
Office: 3 Elyakum Street
PO Box 35238
+ 972-3-688-7691 or +972-9-954-0176,
Fax + 972-3-683-5683
kad_esh@netvision.net.il
Service in Spanish with Hebrew and Russian translation

Kehilat Tel Aviv

(Congregation of Tel Aviv)
Leader: Eli Levi
Phone #: 972-5-449-1539
Email:
el_halev@hotmail.com

Mashiach

Tiferet Yeshua Messianic Congregation (The Glory of Yeshua Messianic Congregation)

Leader: Ari Sorko-Ram
Address: P.O. Box 1414,
Ramat HaSharon 47113
Phone #:   972-3-639-0505
Email:
maozisrael@maozisrael.org
Website:
www.maozisrael.org

Tel Aviv Fellowship

Call for directions
Tel Aviv
Isra'el
Phone: 05-4491539
Services in Hebrew with
Bulgarian translation

Tiberius

Kehilat Peniel The Galilee Experience

Leader: Daniel Yahav
Address: P.O.Box 620
Tiberius 14107
Phone #: 972-4-670-8705
Email:
tsurhaim@netvision.net.il
Services: Shabbat service
Sat. 11am
Hebrew with Russian and
English translation

Morning Star Fellowship

Leader Claude Ezagouri
Phone #: 972 -5-030-5788
Email:
e_claude@netvision.net.il

Messianic Congregations in the
United States & North America

There are several thousand Messianic Congregations throughout the United States, Canada, Mexico & Central America, too many to list separately here. To see a listing of the Messianic Synagogues in your state please go to the **M**essianic **A**llia**N**ce of North America website map:

http://www.man-na.com/

and simply "Click" on the "Messianic Congregation Locator by Country" on the right side of the screen to find a listing of the Synagogues in your city or town.

The **Messianic AlliaNce** of North America exists to provide assistance to those seeking to locate a Messianic Congregation.

Their goal is to promote: Messianic Beliefs, Support of Isra'el, and cooperation between Messianic Congregations world-wide.

Mashiach

Appendix C
Messianic Resources & Links

The resources shown in the following pages and links to Messianic Jewish websites are provided solely as a resource to the reader. The author does not necessarily endorse their individual theology or doctrine.

In recent decades, Messianic Judaism, a movement of Jewish people who have accepted Yeshua as Mashiach and continued to embrace their Jewishness, has been growing steadily. Jews have been coming to faith in Yeshua for centuries, increasingly so after Isra'el became a reality again in the late 1800s with the Zionist movement. After the Holocaust, when Isra'el became a nation again in 1948, the number of Jewish believers in Yeshua has been increasing worldwide, almost in lock step with Jewish immigration to Isra'el.

Messianic Jews are gaining more acceptance in Isra'el. Instead of being perceived as threats to the Isra'elis, due to prejudices going back 2,000 years, they are recognized as friends, fellow citizens, and an active part of Isra'eli society. In part, the groundwork for this was laid by the benevolence work of groups such as Chosen People Ministries, The Joseph Storehouse, the Messianic Jewish Alliance of America's Joseph Project, The International Christian Embassy Jerusalem (ICEJ) and other similar works.

Messianic Resources & Links

Chevra - http://www.chevrahumanitarian.org/

"Chevra (formerly Anshe Rachamim), means friendship. Our goal is to help our people in their time of need. "Chevra is a humanitarian organization, not a religious one. While we help primarily Jewish people, we do not promote religious teaching as a prerequisite or incentive for people to receive our help. Our policy is to informally cooperate with other charities seeking to help Jewish people, but we will help any Jews in need regardless of whether they wish to receive religious information or not.

Chosen People Ministries
http://www.chosenpeople.com/main/

"Chosen People Ministries exists to pray for, evangelize, disciple, and serve Jewish people everywhere and to help fellow believers do the same. The mission was founded in Brooklyn, New York in 1894 by Rabbi Leopold Cohn, a Hungarian Jewish immigrant with a zeal to share the knowledge of Yeshua (Jesus) the Mashiach with G-d's chosen people."

Mashiach

Hashivenu - http://www.hashivenu.org/

"Our goal is a mature Messianic Judaism. We seek an authentic expression of Jewish life maintaining substantial continuity with Jewish tradition. However, Messianic Judaism is energized by the belief that Yeshua of Nazareth is the promised Messiah, the fullness of Torah. Mature Messianic Judaism is not simply Judaism plus Yeshua, but is instead an integrated following of Yeshua through traditional Jewish forms and the modern day practice of Judaism in and through Yeshua."

International Christian Embassy Jerusalem
http://il.icej.org/ - http://us.icej.org/

"The International Christian Embassy was founded in 1980 by evangelical Christians to express their support for the State of Isra'el and the Jewish people. From its inception the ICEJ has had two dominant goals; first, to serve as a conduit of comfort and blessing through which believers in the nations (over 70 today) could show their love and support to Isra'el. Second, the ICEJ stands as a prophetic voice to this generation concerning G-d's unwavering plan to fulfill His covenant promises to the fathers of Isra'el. Namely, that He would ultimately restore the children of Isra'el to their rightful land and sequentially to a right relationship with their G-d, the G-d of Isra'el."

D.A. Osterman

International Messianic Jewish Alliance
http://theimja.org/

"The International Messianic Jewish Alliance (lMJA) is the worldwide fellowship of Jewish people who have accepted Yeshua (Jesus) as their Messiah. It carries out ministries through the work of its affiliated national alliances who unite their efforts to fulfill the aims of the international body."

Jewish Alliance of America's Joseph Project
http://www.mjaa.org/site/PageServer

"The MJAA's Joseph Project is the MJAA's humanitarian aid relief work in Isra'el that has distributed over $100 million in aid to the poor in Isra'el—Jews, Arabs, Muslims, and Christians. The MJAA collects, ships, and distributes more than 75 tons of clothing, furniture, household goods, medical supplies and other aid each year. We distribute this aid through our network of over 35 relief aid centers, along with over 100 other partner Isra'eli organizations and institutes-including Messianic congregations who proclaim Yeshua (Jesus) as the Messiah. Together, we are Jew and Gentile, one in Messiah, working together for the spiritual and physical restoration of Isra'el."

Mashiach

Jews for Jesus - http://www.jewsforjesus.org/

"Jews for Jesus is a Messianic Jewish evangelical organization that focuses on the conversion of the Jewish people to Christianity. Jews for Jesus defines Jewishness in terms of parentage and as a birthright, regardless of religious belief and its members consider themselves to be Jews – either as defined by Jewish law, or according to the view of Jews for Jesus."

Menorah Ministries - http://www.menorah.org/

"Menorah Ministries is an international Messianic missionary ministry of the Gospel to both Jews and Gentiles. We are called to be Front line, personal witnesses, proclaiming the Good News of eternal life through Yeshua, primarily in face-to-face situations. Our reason for existing is not to build our organization, but to glorify G-d through making disciples of Yeshua."

D.A. Osterman

The Association of Messianic Congregations
www.MessianicAssociation.org

The association was formed by leaders in the Messianic Jewish Movement. AMC affiliation is for Messianic Congregations that are Messiah centered, Grace embracing and who value all believers whom G-d has called into His family. AMC desires to encourage Messianic believers to grow in their faith, their walk with Messiah, and their appreciation of G-d's eternal covenant relationship with the Jewish people.

Messianic Isra'el Alliance -
http://www.messianicisrael.com/m/

"Welcome to the Messianic Isra'el Alliance (MIA)--the Voice of Redeemed Isra'el. The Messianic Isra'el Alliance believes Yeshua Ha'Natsree (Jesus of Nazareth) was and is the true Messiah, the Lion of Judah, the Branch Who will fully reunite all Isra'el; that He died and rose from the dead and lives at the right hand of the Almighty; and according to the ancient Holy Scriptures, Genesis to Revelation, Yeshua is YHVH Elohim appearing in the flesh, as Yeshua demonstrated in Himself

232

Mashiach

Messianic Jewish Alliance of America
http://www.mjaa.org/

"The Messianic Jewish Alliance of America is the largest association of *Messianic Jewish* believers in Yeshua (Jesus) in the world. The MJAA is affiliated with Messianic Jewish Alliances in fifteen other countries, including Isra'el."

Tikkun International
http://www.tikkunministries.org/

"Tikkun International is a Messianic Jewish umbrella organization for an apostolic network of leaders, congregations and ministries in covenantal relationship for mutual accountability, support and equipping to extend the Kingdom of G-d in America, Isra'el, and throughout the world."

D.A. Osterman

Union of Messianic Jewish Congregations
http://www.umjc.org/

"The UMJC is the oldest and broadest affiliation of congregations serving the Jewish movement for Yeshua as Mashiach and Lord, serving congregations that are committed to Yeshua and connected with Jewish life and identity. There are some 70 Messianic UMJC Congregations located in North and South America and around the world. We believe that in these latter days, G-d is moving mightily among His Ancient and Holy people, the Jews, bringing the Good News that Mashiach has come."

Vision for Isra'el - https://www.visionforisrael.com/

"At Vision for Isra'el and The Joseph Storehouse, we freely provide aid to the poor and needy people, both Jewish and Arab, living in the nation of Isra'el today."

www.ingramcontent.com/pod-product-compliance
Lightning Source LLC
Chambersburg PA
CBHW070952040426
42443CB00007B/478